1

Jesus Versus Superheroes

The Challenge of Ideas

Darin Simms

Evangel
Publishing House
Nappanee, Indiana

Jesus Versus Superheroes

Evangel Publishing House is an imprint of Simms Publishing Group

Simms Publishing Group
ATTN: Darin Simms
69954 County Road 15
New Paris, IN 46553
Phone: (740) 424-1286
Email: Darin@darinSimms.com
Website: www.darinsimms.com

ISBN-13:
Printed in the United States of America
13 14 15 16 EP 8 7 6 5 4 3 2 1

Dedications and Acknowledgements

Jesus Versus Superheroes is dedicated to the memory of my father, Clifford D. Simms (1935-2013). Thank you, Dad, for introducing me to comic books, for taking me to church, and for encouraging me to pursue my passion for both. You will always be my hero.

I want to thank my wife, Lori, for encouraging me to write and supporting me when she found out I was writing about superheroes. I can do nothing worthwhile without you.

An extra note of thanks to my son, Josiah and his wife, Lauren Simms for their support and encouragement. and Noah Simms. Also, I want to give a special thank you to Hannah Simms for her help in tightening up the manuscript. Abigail Yoder, her husband Lyndon, and their two daughters, Aubrey and Hailey have supported me from day one. And Bethany Simms, thank you for your love and support. You all make be proud to be your father, father-in-law, or grandfather.

Thank you, Deb and Steve Hessler for your encouragement and support. I have always enjoyed the time we spend together, especially when we talk about comic books! Grayson Schmidt was one of the first to support this book and asked nothing in return, I am eternally grateful.

My friends at Union Grove have been overwhelmingly supportive. You have listened to me talk about superheroes for more than a decade. Thank you, Larry and Teresa Fischer, Keith Hartman, Russ and Jenn Price, Darren and Jen Shaw, Duane and Cheryl Stump, Bernie and Violet Weldy, Susanna Weldy, and Margaret Westhafer. A special shout out to Tonya Hunt for all her help.

Aaron Helfer and Kevin Lauer were Superheroes in support of this book. Thank you for believing in me.

My brother Doug Simms, owner of Heroes and Games in the Columbus Convention Center (www.heroes andgames.com) in Columbus, Ohio deserves a thank you for more than just supporting his younger brother. Keep being a hero to so many. My mother, Violet (Gayle) has always shown her love and support for whatever I get myself into. Thanks Mom! My sister Denise (Simms) Sunderland and her husband, Jeff, are great supporters. Thank you for all the ways you have motivated me through the years. To my friends Shawn Armentrout and Jonathan Olvera, thank you for being so gracious to me. I am honored to call you friends.

Dustin Barr, Nathan Culler, Cathy Hahn, Kelly Kern, and Danny Ramirez are golden supporters. Thank you for thinking that I have something interesting to say! I appreciate all of you.

David Amaral, James Conner, Dillon Davis, Teresa Dunham, Tori Dunham, Andrew Needham, Crystal Pamer, Alejandro Rodriguez, Stephany Simms, and Bonnie are great sidekick supporters. Thanks for helping make this a reality.

Daniel Koenig, John Sullivan, ctmoeller, and Frank all gave to help get this book published. I appreciate your faith in me. Thank you!

TABLE OF CONTENTS

Introduction

The Marvel Universe

Stan Lee and Marvel have created some memorable, powerful, and interesting characters over the last fifty plus years. My earliest recollection of reading comics is when I was seven years old. I bought my first Incredible Hulk comic, issue #154. My brother, Doug, and I walked to Risch's Drug Store in Circleville, Ohio. The cover price was just twenty cents. I spent my quarter allowance and rushed home to read what is still one of my favorite stories. That day fanned the spark of superheroes into a flame.

There is a curiosity that comes when you immerse yourself into an imaginary world like the Marvel Universe. I wondered how I would like to live in a world with supervillains, especially if I was without superpowers. I also wondered what would happen if superheroes lived in the real world. Imagining, dreaming, and thinking and then doing it again and again and again. Maybe that is normal for children, but as an adult, thinking through these types of scenarios seems immature. Comparing worlds, reflecting on fictional characters, or wondering if any of what is imagined could become real might be unproductive.

Yet, people invest days, months, and years of their lives in imaginary worlds like the Marvel Universe, the DC Universe, the Walking Dead Universe, the Star Wars Universe, the Harry Potter World, or some other work of fiction. The draw of these imaginary people and places is real and it is powerful.

The Marvel Universe captured me when I was seven and has never let me go. Within that universe there are characters that are older than me, imagined and reimagined by writers and artists, each with their own flair and each with a different slant on the world that is theirs to manipulate. These characters have lived in our minds, in books and literature, and in television and movies. I have wondered what they have to offer the real world.

The Christian Universe

I was raised in a relatively conservative Christian environment where Bible stories were told regularly. Within the pages of the Bible was, perhaps is, a world that I can only imagine. For my curious mind, this world was not unlike the Marvel Universe. Characters seemed heroic or villainous. Some characters performed superhuman acts like defeating a small army with just a jawbone of a donkey.

Imagining, dreaming, and thinking about that world captured my mind. I had hundreds of questions. This Biblical World has had the attention of millions of people for more than a millennia. The Bible was written over hundreds of years by dozens of authors and has remained relatively unchanged since the end of the fourth century C.E.

Unlike comic book writers, Christian scholars and authors do not retell the stories by altering the characters. Some minor characters may be shaded differently by one scholar than another, but the main people remain the same. New characters have not been added.

Research and scholarly studies have illuminated some of the stories and characters. Archeology has helped identify places and dates. The heroics remain attached to the stories. This is part of what makes the Bible so interesting.

Christianity has loved the heroes of the Biblical texts and retold the stories. Those who have heard the stories have marveled at the feats, wondered what life might have been like, and imagined what a future world might be like.

When Universes Collide

The DC Comics era began in 1938 when they published Action Comics 1, the first appearance of Superman. Marvel has it roots in Timely Comics which began in 1939. The Marvel Universe era really does not begin until 1961 when Stan Lee, with assistance from several notable people including Jack Kirby, began telling superhero stories about Spider-Man, Thor, The Hulk, and the Fantastic Four. It did not take long for the DC Universe and the Marvel Universe to collide.

Fans of heroes both companies began to discuss which characters were stronger, faster, and better. Thousands wrote to each company asking for a crossover so fans could see DC heroes interacting with Marvel heroes, fighting each other, and finally defeating a villain worthy of the collaboration. The debate between comic book fans continues today, but in 1976, the two competitors released Superman Versus Spider-Man, the first real crossover between the two universes.

The idea of a crossover between Bible characters and superheroes feels blasphemous from both sides. Nobody wants to see David fighting Thanos or Elijah, the prophet, wearing cape and tights while facing the prophets of Baal. Moses is hero with a cool staff, but not the type of character fans want to see fighting Conan, the Barbarian.

The Christian Universe and the Marvel Universe crossover happened in my mind. I wondered how the characters in the Marvel Universe would see my world. What would they think about Jesus? How do the writers of comic books portray the characters compared to how the writers of the Bible portray Jesus and other characters? Are there similarities in writing styles or genres? I have an expansive list of questions.

When Philosophies Collide

Philosophers, theologians, moral theorists, and scholars postulate ideas and ways of understanding the world. Some of the ideas are more accepted than others. Usually, they posit their ideas in the form of questions. Often, these theories and ideas conflict with one another. One person might suggest that people are inherently good, a second that people are born in sin, while another that good and evil are simply human constructs that have no real definition. These questions inflame debate among scholars and artists alike.

Why is Captain America good? What makes him virtuous? If Doctor Strange can use magic and sorcery for the good of humanity, is he not obligated to do so? Why does Peter Parker carry the burden of responsibility when it comes to stopping crime in his hometown? Why is the Hulk so angry? If anger helps him win, why is it bad? Is it wrong to read about other gods and mythologies? Can a human, empowered by a demon, be a hero?

These questions bring me back to the Bible. Why is Abraham a hero when he gave his wife to another king to safe his own life? Why is David honored when he committed many dishonorable acts? The Apostle Paul killed people for following the teachings of Jesus until he changed his mind and decided to follow those same teachings. We tend to excuse the bad behavior of people we like or idolize. Biblical characters are not exempt from human glosses.

I began comparing the stories I knew from the Bible to the stories I knew from comic books. I began reading what other people wrote as they compared Christian ideas with heroic ideas. *Holy Superheroes!: Exploring the Sacred in Comics, Graphic Novels, and Film* by Greg Garrett (Westminster John Know Press, 2005) and *Who Needs a Superhero: Finding Virtue, Vice, and What's Holy in Comics* by H. Michael Brewer (Baker Books, 2004) were the first two, but many other followed. Some books were about superheroes in general, some touched on just one hero, others were about psychology or philosophy from a superhero perspective, and a few dealt with the genre from its beginning to the time the book was written. None of them satisfied my questioning mind.

That is why I put this book together. I am not trying to validate my Christian beliefs nor am I trying to vilify comic books, comic book writers, or superheroes in general. I do not always hold to Christian orthodoxy (right belief), rather, I posit a way of thinking and living that allows people to wrestle with faith, the Bible, the church, and Christian teachings without being dismissive. On the other hand, I want people to understand that writers create characters and tell stories about those characters that allow the reader to wrestle with that character's life choices. Is it okay for Frank Castle (the Punisher) to kill people he believes have done wrong? As Tony Stark wrestles with alcoholism, is he still a hero? When Spider-Man is unable to save Gwen Stacy, does he become less of a hero?

Faith is not always as certain as Bible teachers, preachers, or professors want us to believe. Comic books are not always as shallow as some would have us believe. Virtue is not exclusive to Christianity. Being heroic is not exclusive to the fictional world of superheroes.

As you read, please keep an open mind. Challenge everything. Wrestle with the ideas. Ask questions. Feel free to disagree. Most of all, enjoy the read. Excelsior!

Chapter 1: Captain America: Freedom, Values, and the American Way

Every person should obey the government in power. No government would exist if it hadn't been established by God. The governments which exist have been put in place by God. Therefore, whoever resists the government opposes what God has established. Those who resist will bring punishment on themselves. People who do what is right don't have to be afraid of the government. But people who do what is wrong should be afraid of it. Would you like to live without being afraid of the government? Do what is right, and it will praise you. The government is God's servant working for your good. But if you do what is wrong, you should be afraid. The government has the right to carry out the death sentence. It is God's servant, an avenger to execute God's anger on anyone who does what is wrong. Therefore, it is necessary for you to obey, not only because you're afraid of God's anger but also because of your own conscience. That is also why you pay your taxes. People in the government are God's servants while they do the work he has given them. Pay everyone whatever you owe them. If you owe taxes, pay them. If you owe tolls, pay them. If you owe someone respect, respect that person. If you owe someone honor, honor that person. Pay your debts as they come due. However, one debt you can never finish paying is the debt of love that you owe each other. The one who loves another person has fulfilled Moses' Teachings. The commandments, "Never commit adultery; never murder; never steal; never have wrong desires," and every other commandment are summed up in this statement: "Love your neighbor as you love yourself." Love never does anything that is harmful to a neighbor. Therefore, love fulfills Moses' Teachings. https://my.bible.com/bible/70/ROM.13.1-10

What it means to be American

In the United States, there is an assumption that only people who live in the USA are Americans, different from those who live in Canada or Mexico or Brazil. So, what constitutes being American? What are the values Americans are supposed to hold? What symbols do we use to represent America? Most importantly, how do American values line up with Christian values?

Captain America

Captain America, aka Steve Rogers, is an iconic figure in pop culture and in American pulp literature. He represents something of all the values that America prizes; courage, humility, confidence, leadership, nobility, honesty, and a conviction to do the right thing (even when it is difficult). He values freedom, individualism, and trust in government. Many of these traits and values he is either born with or he learns them from his family. Others he picks up and develops throughout his life.

World War II began in September 1939 when Germany invaded Poland. In early 1941, the creators of Captain America, Jack Kirby and Joe Simon, wanted a character that could be an iconic figure. More than iconic, they wanted this him to inspire Americans and those serving in the Armed Forces to do what was necessary to win the war. They were looking to create a character to rally the American spirit.

In New York, where Kirby and Simon worked and lived, there seemed to be a resistance to the war. Many politicians spoke against getting involved. There was a lingering doubt about the value of war in Europe. To make a statement, Kirby and Simon draw a spectacular and controversial cover for issue number one dated March 1941, showing Captain America punching Adolph Hitler square in the jaw. This is the beginning of the rise of a hero.

(For more detailed information on this time period go to https://encyclopedia.ushmm.org/content/en/article/the-united-states-isolation-intervention or https://www.nationalww2museum.org/war/articles/great-debate). The United States would not enter the war until December 1941 after the Japanese bombed of Pearl Harbor.

After the war, Captain America's popularity began to fade. A war hero did not seem to fit in to a post-war America. There was no evil nation to fight, no need to rally the troops, and no interest in reliving the past. Sales dropped so drastically that in 1954, the Captain America comic book is cancelled at issue 78. For the next ten years no one hears about Captain America until, in 1964, Stan Lee decides to revive the character. He has been around ever since, and the world is better for it. Captain America presents a unique form of nationalism.

The big question is, how does American nationalism, as depicted in Captain America, compare to the teachings of Jesus and Christianity? Let's check out Captain America first.

Out of His Time

Understand that Captain America is a man out of his time. In the 1964 return, Stan Lee tells the story of Steve Rogers crashing a plane in the Arctic Ocean. Because of the Super Soldier Serum that turned him into Captain America, his body freezes in the ice and is preserved. When they find him decades later (in the Marvel Cinematic Universe it is nearly 50 years later) and thaw him, he is able to recover completely. However, everyone he knew before is gone. The world has changed, and he was not a part of the change. His past life is gone and his present holds little that is recognizable. His environment has changed. Technology has changed. He has not.

Without Purpose

Not only is he a man outside of his time, but he is also a man without purpose. Steve Rogers wanted to fight in WWII. He was a soldier. In 1964 (comics) or 2011 (movie) there is no war for him. His entire purpose for living, to rid the world of Hitler and fascism, has all but disappeared. He does not fight in Vietnam or the Iraq/Afghanistan conflict. He has no obvious way to use his gifts and talents in a world so dissimilar to what he knows. So much time has passed that he has no purpose in this new era.

Without Friends

Steve Rogers is also a man without friends. In 1964, everyone he would have known had aged, changed, died, or moved on with their lives. His family is gone. Since he never married, there is no one for him to go home to. If it's 2011, everyone is dead or elderly, ninety something. He is alone in a world not his own without purpose or direction. It may be that his country is all that remains for him. He represents a passion for freedom and independence, a sense of individualism, and a trust in government (equity under the law).

If you have ever felt any of these feelings, out of time, without purpose, and/or without friends, then you understand Steve Rogers, and perhaps this is what connects you to Captain America and his American values. Looking at these three values can help us understand what it means to be an American.

Freedom

Freedom means that a person is unrestrained, able to do whatever said person wishes to do. In the United States, people are not entirely free. We are restrained by government regulations, laws, and ordinances. We are not free to do whatever we want. However, as Americans, we value freedom. We want to be free. The nation was designed for people to be self-governed. That is real freedom. It is a belief that people do not need a government or a monarch to tell them what they can or cannot, should or should not, must or must not do. Americans should be a group of self-governing people.

In contemporary political discussions, almost no one talks about the value of freedom as self-governance. People in power do not trust you to make the decisions that they think you should make. It is not that they do not trust you to make good decisions, it is that they do not trust you to make the decisions that they want you to make. They believe they know more than you, they know better than you, and they are smarter than you.

Every law that is passed, every regulation that is enacted, and every executive order signed is another limit to freedom and independence. Every law limits what you can do. With each limit, your freedom is restricted. Legislators prefer compliance to their will rather than supporting the freedoms and liberties of their constituents. If you comply with those in authority, your life will be better.

As you read Romans 13, you notice that Paul does not say anything about independence or freedom in connection to governments. He tells the readers in Rome to obey their leaders because government is God's tool. Paul goes as far to suggest that anyone who resists governmental authority is resisting God and deserving of condemnation.

Individualism

The second American value embodied by Captain America is individualism. Individualism means that you are not dependent on anyone else for your own well-being. You do not depend on assistance from government agencies, charitable organizations, or people in authority for your family's well-being. Today's political climate encourages people to depend on government agencies. Politicians openly invite people to use government services, to expand government services, and to include as many people as possible in the government services.

Most of these government services were intended to assist Americans for a brief time until they could get back on their feet. It has become a way of life and an expectation. There are people on welfare assistance for three and four generations. They have sacrificed their independence for a pittance from Uncle Sam. Far too many retire and live off of their Social Security, even though the program was meant to be an assistance to retirement rather than a person's entire income during retirement. Is it possible that Americans today do not value independence? Or, is it possible that those in government want to make citizens more and more dependent on government?

Individualism thinks differently than Paul. Individualists make their own way, build their own roads, clear their own land, grow their own food, and so much more. They struggle and labor to make their lives what they want it to be. They may ask a neighbor for assistance or help a neighbor who needs assistance, but they will ultimately take responsibility for the outcomes for their own decisions. They pick themselves up when they fall, they find determination and motivation within themselves, and they empower themselves to do what needs to be done. The rugged individualist will find a way to accomplish whatever needs to be done, with or without government permission or sanction.

There are there things you cannot do, of course. Some things you are not physically capable of doing, some things you are not mentally capable of doing, and other things you are not allowed to do legally and/or morally. The individualist will always figure out a way to get something done if deemed necessary. That is something of great value to the American spirit.

Captain America is an individualist. Yes, he works well with others, but each person on his team must have his or her own objective. He gets things done and he does them "the right way." He does not let obstacles, no matter how daunting, prevent him from achieving his goal or mission. That seems admirable and respectable.

In today's culture, individualism is uncommon. People want government to do things for them, to make life easier for them, and to give them things they could get for themselves with some time and effort. Politicians pander to their constituents and try to provide as much as they can from the public dole.

Equality Under the Law

This is the most important American value. All people should be held equally responsible under the law. The founders wanted to make sure that all Americans were protected legally. The poor should have legal counsel as well as the rich. Wealth should not lessen the penalties of breaking the law. Equality under the law protects the poor, the people on the fringes of society, and those with less social stature. It also holds the wealthy accountable.

It is true that throughout American history, not all people have been treated fairly regarding the legal system. Those who have needed legal protection have not received it. Those who should have had legal charges brought against them have been allowed to skate through. Some people have had the force of law brought against them unjustly. Every time this happens, it weakens the fabric of our culture. Equality under the law means that if you break a law and I break the same law, the legal system should treat us the same way. Power, position, and wealth should have nothing to do with jurisprudence.

Captain America understands this. He values the equality of all humans. He especially understands how governments and law enforcement can overstep and mistreat or abuse the people they are supposed to protect. In Captain America: Civil War, he takes a stand against the government when they want all beings with "super" powers to register with a government agency. Captain America thinks each super-powered person can manage himself or herself. They should not be treated differently under the law than other humans. Freedom, individualism, and equality were all at play in the story.

Teaching of Jesus

In Galatians 5:13, Paul wrote,

"You were indeed called to be free, brothers and sisters. Don't turn this freedom into an excuse for your corrupt nature to express itself. Rather, serve each other through love." (https://my.bible.com/bible/70/GAL.5.13)

Too often, we think the United States was so perfectly designed that everything about it lines up with the teachings of Jesus. We seldom look at the teachings of Jesus and American values at the same time with discerning eyes. The challenge here is to see if freedom, individualism, and equality under the law are Christian values or simply good political practice. Could it be that Jesus has a different way of looking at culture?

This idea of freedom, free to do whatever I want to do, gets muddled by Paul when he tells the believers in Galatia that while you are indeed called to be free, it is not a license to do whatever you want whenever you want. Your freedom is limited, not by the law, not by tradition, not but government, not by cultural expectations, but by your capacity for loving others. You are free to do whatever you want if that will serve other people. This is a different way of thinking about freedom. You are free to serve people in any way that you want so long as it communicates love to them. You are free to look after the well-being of someone else, all the time, no restrictions.

We think of freedom as being able to do whatever we want to do, whatever brings us benefit or happiness. Paul thinks differently. As he writes to this church, he tells them not to use their freedom as an excuse for your corrupt nature to express itself. What he means by "corrupt nature" is selfishness. Paul insists that you are free to do whatever you want as long as it serves somebody other than yourself. This is Christian freedom.

Individualism is an American value as previously discussed. The right of the individual, the power to self-determine your life, and the resolve to take care of you and yours first and foremost. However, Jesus taught about being one among many. Paul writes about this idea in Philippians 2, which is one of the most beautifully written passages in all of the New Testament.

1 So then, as Christians, do you have any encouragement? Do you have any comfort from love? Do you have any spiritual relationships? Do you have any sympathy and compassion? 2 Then fill me with joy by having the same attitude and the same love, living in harmony, and keeping one purpose in mind. 3 Don't act out of selfish ambition or be conceited. Instead, humbly think of others as being better than yourselves. (https://my.bible.com/bible/70/PHI.5.1-3)

Paul says that you are important, but not more important than anybody else. In verse 5, he tells them to consider the life of Jesus as an example. Jesus lived a life that gave to other people constantly, to the point where he died on a cross for the benefit of other people. Jesus did not get anything out of his life on earth. Jesus did not get anything out of being humiliated and nailed to a cross. It did not benefit him at all. Paul says that should be your example, that is how you should live your life. That is not American individualism.

The third value is equality under the law. While we speak of the rule of law and equality under the law in American values, Jesus taught about being free from the law. So, when we hear the word "freedom," we should think about freedom from the law and interpreting laws within this freedom.

In his sermon on the mount in Matthew 5, Jesus says he came, not to abolish the law, but to fulfill the law. Specifically, he is referencing the Old Testament Law. What does it mean to fulfill a law? There is a difference between getting rid of a law and fulfilling a law. Understanding that difference is indispensable to understanding Jesus. Jesus is not teaching that we should be lawless or that each person should do what they think is right. We should not be lawless. Instead, Jesus says he fulfilled all the requirements of the law, therefore we are no longer bound by to that law. In our selfishness, we think that means we do whatever we want. We think like children. We can drive as fast as we want, eat as much as we want, drink as much as we want, we can do whatever we want, whenever we want, for as long as we want. That is lawlessness, not law fulfillment. In Romans 8, Paul says specifically that it is *love* that fulfills the law. Love never does anything that harms another. That is how love fulfills the law. It is an incredible message!

We want to talk about freedom and liberty and independence. We want to do what we want when we want. We want to make our own decisions, make our own rules, create our own lives, and manifest our own destinies. Jesus' teaching is a little different than that. We are still free from the law. We are not bound to it anymore. All the laws in scripture can be summed up in a phrase, "Love your neighbor as yourself."

Jesus said it in the sermon on the mount in Matthew 7. Paul wrote it in Galatians chapter 5. John wrote it in 1 John. Peter wrote in 1 Peter that the law is fulfilled in loving other people, not in doing whatever we want. Liberty is found when we serve one another, not when we serve our own self interests. And while you need to take care of yourself, it is not taking care in a self-interested way. Loving your neighbor as yourself means that you take care of yourself and you take care of others. Maybe, you take care of yourself *as* you take care of others. This does not suggest neglecting yourself. If you did that, you would be neglecting your neighbor as well. You will do to your neighbor what you do for yourself.

It is important for you to take care of yourself. It is important to work at understanding how to love others. It is important for you to follow the teachings of Jesus, but only to the extent that in so doing, you benefit somebody else, not so you get the benefit of getting to heaven. That was not the teaching of Jesus. The teaching of Jesus is that you should follow Jesus' example so that you can benefit others. The reward for doing that is heaven, but it isn't the purpose for doing it. Your following Jesus is designed entirely for you to benefit other people in this life. You are free to do whatever you want as long as it serves others.

Serve your family. Serve your significant other. Serve your mother or father. Serve the person who lives in the house next to you. Serve the people that work with you. Look after their best interests. This is the teaching of Jesus. It is a little different than American values. Do you identify more with American values and Captain America or with the teachings of Jesus?

Chapter 2: Spider-Man: With Great Power

You received a gift from God when I placed my hands on you [to ordain you]. Now I'm reminding you to fan that gift into flames. God didn't give us a cowardly spirit but a spirit of power, love, and good judgment.
(https://my.bible.com/bible/70/2TI.1.6-7)

"With great power comes great responsibility." Uttered by Peter Parker's Uncle Ben, these words become the anchor to hold Spider-Man to a moral center. Finding a moral center and having moral clarity is not an easy task. With Spider-Man, we have an opportunity to look at the need for moral clarity and how to shape moral clarity and then compare that with the teachings of Jesus.

Morality is a standard of right and wrong or proper and improper behavior. It may or may not incorporate religious values, societal values or norms, and instinctual virtues or principles. In most (and especially early) superhero stories, the heroes are expected to behave heroically, with high virtue and integrity, to do right, and to be exemplary human beings. Even in modern culture, we expect these attributes, appropriately or not, from our first responders, law enforcement, military personnel, and to some extent, politicians, teachers, and educators. As a society, we feel a breach of trust when we read or hear of stories of misbehavior from people in these professions if, in their professional capacity, they behave outside the heroic norm (think teachers who have affairs with students, dirty cops, deceitful politicians, or rogue military members).

Imagine a superhero world where those with superpowers used them for their own good and rarely took time or interest in helping others. Would it be wrong for a super-powered person to not use his or her powers to help others? Could that person help others and take advantage of their powers to help themselves as well? Could they work for hire (see Luke Cage: Hero for Hire) and still be considered virtuous? Could they work against governments to topple leaders they feel are unworthy of the leadership position? These are moral questions with answers that are not as clear as we would hope. Finding answers for our real world will be even more difficult but looking at the Spider-Man story may help.

Beginnings

Peter Parker was just a high school student on a field trip to a science exhibition when a radioactive spider bit him. Little did he know that that one moment would forever change the course of his rather unremarkable life. The spider bite gave Peter remarkable abilities; tacky touch that allows him to climb any solid object without falling, a spider sense to warn him of danger, and super strength.

Unsure what he could or should do with his new found power, Peter decides to put on a mask and wrestle Crusher Hogan for a sizable cash prize. After winning the match, Peter buys the materials he needed to construct his web-shooters.

He has no plans to do anything virtuous with his powers, Peter only wants to improve his life and that of his Aunt May and Uncle Ben, who became Peter's parental figures after an accident killed his mother and father.

After one match that Peter wins, he heads backstage to collect his winnings. However, another man is there to rob the promoter when Peter arrives and because Peter does not particularly like the promoter, he allows the robber to escape with the money. Coincidentally, the robber makes his way to Uncle Ben and in the confrontation kills Peter's uncle. When Peter finds out that his uncle's murderer was the same man he refused to stop at the wresting event, he learns that "At least in this world, with great power, there must also come great responsibility." This line has rung true for Spider-Man, for Peter Parker, and for comic book fans from 1962 until today.

Jesus

The story of Jesus can be told as a superhero story. Jesus has great power because he is the son of God. He lays his power aside and comes to earth to be born as a human in a cave near Bethlehem, among animals, and wrapped in rags, to parents who were poor and considered outcasts among their own family. Jesus has to figure out how to live without any powers, as someone who once had unlimited powers but now has nothing.

Jesus is the opposite of Peter Parker. Peter was born without much in life and gets powers that he must learn to live with. Jesus was eternal and must learn to live a limited existence. We do not have much information about Jesus' childhood and what we do have is not particularly reliable. So, we look to the Gospels to see how the adult Jesus is getting along.

In one passage, we read about Jesus walking on water (Mark 6, John 6, and Matthew 12). This seems odd to us today and many theologians struggle with it as well. The son of God who gave up his godhood (Philippians 1-2) to come to earth somehow has powers to defy natural law. Many believe he received the power to do miracles, heal the sick, and cast out demons when he was baptized (Mark 1, Matthew 3, Luke 3). Others say it is his godly powers that allow him to warp the laws of science. Regardless, this power that Jesus has is being used to benefit others. Jesus knew that his power brought with it great responsibility. For about three years, Jesus goes about preaching the good news and using his power to help those in need. He teaches about God's kingdom and how its kingdom can change their lives. He states that there is power in God's kingdom (Mark 9:1). This good news can provide his followers with power to change their lives, the lives of people they know, and even the entire world (Acts 1:8).

In Paul's second letter to Timothy, he writes,

You received a gift from God when I placed my hands on you [to ordain you]. Now I'm reminding you to fan that gift into flames. God didn't give us a cowardly spirit but a spirit of power, love, and good judgment. So never be ashamed to tell others about our Lord or be ashamed of me, his prisoner.

Instead, by God's power, join me in suffering for the sake of the Good News (https://my.bible.com/bible/70/2TI.1.6-8).

It is interesting that Paul uses the word power because most of us as followers of Jesus do not feel like we have much power. We feel like God has all the power or Jesus has all the power or the Holy Spirit has all the power. We do not have much, if any, power. But that is not what Paul says. Paul tells Timothy that he has this power and Paul is going to tell him how to be responsible with it.

What was Jesus' responsibility to humanity? When you consider the life of Jesus, what was he responsible for, what did he need to do? Why was it his job to take all that was wrong with the world and put it on himself? For most of us, we do not want to take responsibility for our own faults or shortcomings, let alone the faults and shortcomings of others. Jesus comes to earth, without the power of God, and says that he will take responsibility for every human's faults. The stories we have about Jesus are designed for us to learn how to be responsible with the power he has given us.

Your Power and Responsibility

Peter Parker takes the name Spider-Man because his powers came from a spider. His name represents where his power originates. So, when followers of Jesus Christ take the name Christian, we are representing the origin of our power, Jesus. As Peter Parker emulates a spider, Christians should emulate Christ, or Jesus. Peter went from a weak boy to a super-powered man via a spider bite. Christians are going from a normal human existence to a love-powered existence via a crucified savior. Both the spider and the Christ lost their lives to empower another; the spider for one person, the Christ for all people. Peter Parker is given power to change his life. Christians, meaning "little Christs," were given power to change the world.

With that power comes great responsibility. Paul tries to explain to Timothy that he has a great responsibility as a follower of Christ. God has not given us a spirit of timidity, a power to shrink back, or a power to stand aside. Rather, Paul says God has given us the spirit of power and of love and of a sound mind. Those three things become tremendously important.

Your Story

What you need to know first is that you have a story. You may not know your story yet, but you, undoubtedly, have a story. You have a story about how you came to know the power of God in your life. Some may say, "I have never seen or experienced the power of God" or "God has never changed me" or "I know a story about God, but no personal experience with that God." That, too, is a story.

Of all the hero stories that you can read, and there are thousands, the story of Jesus should make us stop and think about what our responsibility is with the power that God has given to us. What is your part in the story? You should have your own origin story that explains how God came into your life.

Spider-Man has been around since 1962 and there have been hundreds of Spider-Man stories told over the decades in comics, in novels, in television shows, in cartoons, in movies, and in fan fiction. Why do we have such a difficult time finding our own story? Maybe it is because we do not accept the power that God gave us, or we only hope to use it for ourselves rather than for the benefit of our world.

The truth is you are probably not going to walk on water. You are probably not going to be the person who touches the sick and heals them. You are probably not going to be someone who casts out demons. You are probably not going to feed thousands of people with a few loaves of bread and a couple of fishes. That is not what you have been called to do. But you have been given a power to change the world.

Paul clearly tells Timothy that he, and therefore you, has the power of love and a sound mind. And if you will use those powers, if you will understand these two things, you will understand Jesus and you can change the world. You can save the world.

You are not going to rid the world of evil. You are not going to put an end to violence and hatred. However, you can change a person. You have the power to change the life of somebody you know by loving them in a way they have never understood before. The power of love that Jesus showed us, as demonstrated in the Gospels, is that we do not follow Christ because we have a list of rules to follow. We follow Jesus so we can show people what it means to love, to put other people first, and to put ourselves behind those other people.

As Peter Parker gets older, he realizes how important it is to put his own needs and fears aside to rescue other human beings. He puts their safety ahead of his own, their need to survive ahead of his own, and even their pursuit of happiness ahead of his own. Often that means that he does not get what he wants.

One of the most poignant stories in the Spider-Man collection is the story of Peter's love of Gwen Stacy. It is a story written by Gerry Conaway in 1973 (see Amazing Spider-Man 121 and 122) and it shook the comic world. Peter and Gwen were desperately in love and one of Spider-Man's enemies, the Green Goblin, knew it. He captured Gwen and in an opportune moment in the fight with Spider-Man, the Goblin throws Gwen from a bridge. Spider-Man attempts to rescue her, but when he spins a web to catch her as she's hurtling towards the ground, he hears her neck snap, and she is dead. Hero stories are not supposed to end like that. Peter, Spider-Man is supposed to save her, to rescue her, to be her hero.

There is something about being a hero, about being a person with the power to change someone's life for the better, when the hero gets hurt as much or more than the person being rescued. It is true for us too. In your effort to change and help other people to have a better life, you often get hurt and things around you do not go well. We do not think about following Christ like that.

Paul goes on to tell Timothy that if he understands the power of love and a sound mind that he will have to understand suffering. As much as we try to love people, evil will still be there. You will not be exempt from pain or sorrow. That is one of the most disappointing things about being a Christian. I think it is one of the most disappointing things about being a hero. You will get hurt. You may be devastated. There is evil in the world. There are people who will take advantage of your goodness, or only look out for their own interests, or who will put you and your loved ones in peril intentionally. No matter how hard you try to love them, they will not accept it.

What Paul tells Timothy is not to let that stop you. Join in the suffering of Christ because you can change the world. You have the power. And with that power comes responsibility. For many, we grew up in churches where we had no responsibilities other than to tell stories about Jesus and his followers, to recite and enact those stories or to pray for one another. But the message of Jesus was not that his followers would recite stories over and over again. The message of Jesus was not that his followers would spend hours a day praying for one another and laying our needs at the foot of the cross. The message of Jesus was not that his followers would sing songs about how great God is and how much we love God.

The power that God has given us, the power of love and a sound mind, is so that we could go out and save the world one person at a time. It is a great responsibility. Not everyone is willing to do it, but if you are going to be a follower of Christ, you have to do it. You have a responsibility with the power that God has given you to go out and change the world. Think through what is going on in your life and find ways to love people that will break the norms they are used to seeing. Put other people's interests ahead of your own. Put their well-being ahead of your own. Create for them a place where they can be accepted for who they are. Love them, even if you think they are evil.

One thing we know about Peter Parker is that, with all the villains he faces, he not only tries to rescue the innocents, but to change the evil that he sees. He does not hate the villains although he hates what they do and the chaos and destruction they cause. He uses his power and his mind to attempt to convince then to stop doing evil. That is our responsibility.

Do you consider yourself a hero? You have a chance to change the life of someone you know. With the power God has given you, you can rescue people from their fears; the fear of being alone, the fear of being rejected, the fear of being misunderstood. You have that power. What will you do with it?

Chapter 3: The Hulk: Controlling the Rage Within

Remember this, my dear brothers and sisters: Everyone should be quick to listen, slow to speak, and should not get angry easily. An angry person doesn't do what God approves of. https://my.bible.com/bible/70/JAS.1.19-20

What makes you angry, so angry you could spit? What is it that sends you into a rage? How do you, then, handle that anger and rage? Do you know anyone who has anger issues? In a culture where being outraged is a daily occurrence, is there a good way to deal with our anger? How does the Hulk deal with anger and how does Jesus deal with anger? Who has the better way?

All of us have been angry! While some people may be more angry or angry more than others, sadly, anger is far too familiar an experience for all of us. It is also true that each person expresses anger differently, and many of us have, once or twice, had our anger turn into rage, saying and/or doing things that we regret having said or done. Anger has a way of bringing out the worst in humanity and that leads us to the Hulk.

Beginnings

In 1962, Stan Lee and Jack Kirby told a story about a physicist, Dr. Bruce Banner. Banner is part of a military team that designs and builds bombs. One fateful day, Banner is preparing to test a gamma bomb when he notices a young man, Rick Jones, has entered the test area. Unable to stop the bomb launch, Banner races off to the site to rescue the wayward Jones. Banner is able to get his young friend to safety, but he cannot get himself to safety. When the explosion happens, Banner is bombarded with gamma rays. The gamma rays change Banner so that when he gets angry, Banner disappears, and the Hulk emerges. As the Hulk, Banner cannot contain or control his behaviors. It is still Banner's brain, though in primitive form, in the Hulk's body and he can remember everything the Hulk does. He knows the pain and destruction that result from his monstrous rage.

As a result, Banner spends the rest of his life trying to rid himself of the monster that dwells within him. He wants to find a way to control the Hulk, or better yet, to rid himself of the Hulk. The Hulk is uncontrollable. Banner lived his life in control. The Hulk lives without control. The tension between the two is real. Banner is a genius. The Hulk is primal and can barely put sentences together.

Banner is powerless as a human but powerful as the Hulk. Banner works a job where he is always the smartest person in the room but does not get to make decisions. His insights are often discarded or ignored. He has no power or control over his job. People are telling him what to do even when they have no understanding of what he does. He is frustrated by the red tape and administrative barriers to doing the right things. He feels powerless.

As the Hulk, Banner feels powerful. Even though the Hulk destroys property and harms people (although often unintentionally), a part of Banner likes the feeling he gets from being strong, powerful, and invulnerable. The government puts General Thaddeus "Thunderbolt" Ross in charge of keeping the Hulk in check, preventing the Hulk from destroying property or hurting people. But even a general with weapons and troops in abundance cannot contain the rampaging Hulk. In his rage, the Hulk often hurts the people that Banner loves, including the general's daughter, Betty Ross. It seems nothing can stop the Hulk. The angrier he gets, the stronger he gets, and the more destructive he gets. People fear the monster.

Lee and Kirby tapped into the real issue with rage and anger when they created the Hulk. People who have anger issues often recognize that they need to do something about it. They want to stop being angry, but they cannot seem to control it. Often, it is the times in our lives when we are frustrated or feel powerless that anger takes control of us. The anger makes us feel strong and powerful. When people are angry, they often hurt the people they love and damage property and possessions. The angry person becomes a monster that other people are afraid of. And people who are angry do not do what God wants.

In the 1970's television series, Banner, played by Bill Bixby, utters this iconic line to an investigative reporter, "Mr. McGee, don't make me angry. You wouldn't like me when I'm angry." The truth is that it is difficult to know what makes someone angry. It is also true that we do not like most angry people. What makes you angry?

Anger

A common thing that makes us anger is exasperation with people of circumstances. We get exasperated with people when they do or say things that make life more difficult for us. Some will turn that frustration into snarkiness, but many get angry. Why can't they get it right? Why do I have to keep repeating myself? Why do people have to be so stupid? Why are they doing that to me? Why are they trying to control me? We get irritated or annoyed and the next thing you know, we're angry! Our exasperation with people and/or the circumstances of life can enrage us.

When we make numerous attempts to change things and nothing changes, we can get angry. We know something is not right or a relationship is not right, and we attempt to fix it over and over, but nothing gets better. We feel exasperated! Why can't we get this right? Why can't they figure that out? Why can't they just do what I tell them or do what I need them to do? Our exasperation quickly turns to anger.

Constant nagging and annoying can lead us to get angry too. Or, when people are always chirping in our ears telling us what they want us or need us to do, we can get annoyed. For example, when your boss, who sits in his office all day doing who knows what, tells you what he needs you to do before he leaves for the day. He does not care what else is on your task list, he just wants what he wants. Or, when your dad tells you every ten minutes to take out the trash or your mom reminds you to pick up your dirty clothes or your significant other tells you fifty times that the yard needs mowed. You are probably feeling exasperated now just from reading this paragraph. It does not take much for that exasperation to turn to anger.

When people say mean or critical things to you unexpectedly, it can set you off. This happens often in families. You know the buttons to push to irritate someone in your family. There are people in your family that you know how to push their buttons and make them angry. When people act suddenly or unexpectedly with either verbal attacks or physical assaults, or some behavior that seems way out of line, we get angry. "What in the world are you doing? Stop acting that way! Stop saying that!" Our volume raises, our pitch raises, our tone changes, and our speech quickens. Suddenly, we are angry!

Power

Our anger is closely linked to power just as it is with the Hulk. What happens when we get angry is that we use our anger to take power in a conflict. So, if we're having a conflict with someone, a husband or wife or son or daughter or mother or father or co-worker or boss or neighbor, and we feel like you do not have power, just like Bruce Banner felt like he had no power, anger makes us feel invulnerable. We cannot be hurt. When we are angry, we have that moment when we do not think anything anyone says or does can hurt us. Further, it does not matter what we say or do because we have the power in that moment. We want that sense of power and control. We like feeling invulnerable.

We not only feel invulnerable; we also feel invincible. We feel like we can do anything. We will take on the world when we are angry. If the whole family wants to fight us, bring it on! It is that sense that nothing can beat us, no person can beat us, and no group of people can beat us. This leads us to that place where we lose control.

If we are being honest, it is that uncontrollable rage that feels so good. The brain releases chemicals into the body including adrenaline, dopamine, and cortisol, helping us to feel strong and invulnerable. It feels good to let the rage out. It feels good to say the things we have always wanted to say. It feels good to be out of control for a moment and to not concern ourselves with the consequences of our behavior or the consequences of our words. It gives us a sense of strength and power. And that feels very good.

The truth is that anger is just another form of selfishness. It is a base desire to have our own way. It is designed in our DNA for self-preservation to want our way most of the time, if not all the time. Our primary instinct is to take care of our self. It is difficult for us to give up what we want for someone else's good. When we really want something, it is hard to say "No, I do not have to have that."

When we want to be right, we need to be right and it is hard to say, "I do not have to be right this time, even though I am right." We cannot say, I do not have to win this argument" because we think we always have to win. Nobody wants to lose. What happens is that our base desire to have our way fuels our anger. It is a sense of selfishness, a sense of self-importance that gets us to rage.

Anger gives us a sense of superiority over others. When we're angry and we can yell louder than someone else, and we can be bigger than them, and we can be stronger than them, and we can read the riot act to them and they cannot do anything about it, it gives us a sense of power and satisfaction. We feel superior to them and that feels good to us.

Even more, when we are angry, we feel a sense of self-sufficiency. We do not need anyone else. You have probably said something like that when you have been angry. "Go ahead! Leave! I don't care! I don't need you! I don't need anyone! I don't need your time! I don't need your money. I don't need your help! I don't need your love! Go ahead and walk out, I don't care!" Anger makes us think we are okay by ourselves. We are not okay by ourselves, but in our anger and rage we feel like we are. It is odd what we will believe in our anger and rage. The Hulk often tells people to go away because he does not need them, does not want them, does not need anyone. He is wrong. Banner desires love and connection more than anything. It just escapes him and his inner monster drives people who could love him away from him.

Jesus

Look at how Jesus dealt with anger. There are stories in the Bible where Jesus is angry, but he directs his anger at unrighteous situations. He does not lash out at people directly. The first story can be found in John chapter two beginning with verse thirteen. It is an interesting passage because Matthew, Mark, and Luke tell a similar story, but place it in a different context (see Matthew 21:12-13, Mark 11:15-17, and Luke 19:45-46). In this story, Jesus enters the temple in Jerusalem and begins turning over tables and driving the money changers out of the temple. John's account says he made a whip and drove out the people as well as the animals. His disciples remembered a passage from Psalm 69 that says the messiah will have a zeal or devotion for God's house, the temple. Jesus says to those selling the animals and birds that they are using the temple for making money and that was not the purpose of the temple.

As a little background, the Jews were still offering animal sacrifices for the forgiveness of sins and other religious rituals during this time. What animal you offered was based on your social status. The wealthier you were, the more you could afford, the bigger animal you had to offer. So, if you were poor and did not have your own farm or did not own animals you could buy an animal from the temple store. If you were wealthy, this would not matter to you. You could bring one of your own animals or pay the going rate for one at the temple. But for the poor, the money changers would over charge the price on the low-end birds or animals because they knew people had to have them to get their sins forgiven. It always took advantage of the poor. When Jesus comes in, he says, in essence, "Enough of this! Stop taking advantage of the poor! The temple is not supposed to be like this! You are not supposed to be taking advantage of people. It is intended to be a house of prayer." He tips over the tables and tells them to leave. He was angry, but he directed his anger at the situation, not at the people. He wanted to reform what was being done in the temple, not destroy the people who were there or the temple itself.

The second story comes from Matthew chapter twenty-three. Jesus rants against the Pharisees, the religious leaders of the day. He calls them whitewashed tombstones, pristine on the outside but dead on the inside. He says they are blind leaders who take advantage of widows and the poor. They are like a cup that is clean on the outside but filthy on the inside. He calls them poisonous snakes and hypocrites who would strain gnats but swallow camels. Jesus words are harsh, but he is not angry at any particular person. He was angry about how the religious culture had developed where what mattered most was how you appear on the outside rather than how you really are inwardly. That situation is still with us today. Jesus rants against the Pharisees but does not allow his anger to destroy them.

Actually, Jesus goes to the cross to be executed for the very people he is ranting against. Even though he tells them that he is going to destroy the temple structure, not physically, but the religious culture and practice, he is crucified so they can have a new understanding of how God works. Jesus absorbs God's wrath or anger on behalf of other people.

God tells Jesus, I want you to go live a life among people you do not know, among people who you are not like, and among people who will not like you. In the end, they will beat you, they will insult you, spit on you and then nail your flesh to a tree. Although you may have power to change any of that, I do not want you to lift a finger because I am going to pour out my anger (wrath) toward their sin (selfishness) on you.

How exciting is that plan for Jesus? Can you imagine Jesus saying, "Sounds like a great plan, I'm all in. How soon can we start?" What Jesus did was absorb God's anger not for his benefit, but for our benefit. Jesus could have been angry at his father for even suggesting it, but instead, he sees the benefit of helping people rather than getting angry. He could have been angry with humanity for their inability to understand love and selflessness. Instead, he faces is predicament with humility and grace.

In Matthew 5:21-24, Jesus teaches:

"You have heard that it was said to your ancestors, 'Never murder. Whoever murders will answer for it in court.' But I can guarantee that whoever is angry with another believer will answer for it in court.
(https://my.bible.com/bible/70/MAT.5.21-24)

If you are angry with your brothers or sister, the people who live in your own house, the people you worship with,

Jesus says your guilty. We do not like to hear that because we like the power of feeling angry. Like Bruce Banner, we like feeling the rage inside us. We like feeling powerful in moments when we are powerless. Jesus was not like that.

Prayer and Meditation

Jesus used prayer and meditation in ways that we do not take advantage of. One of the things Jesus did was to find time for solitude. When was the last time you went off by yourself for an extended time, more than an hour, for the purpose of spiritual insight or renewal? I am guessing never. Or, if you have done it, you cannot remember. You may go on couple's retreats or men's retreats, or women's retreats, or youth camp, but never alone. You probably like to have other people around you, especially on spiritual or religious experiences. Jesus thought it necessary to find solitude.

It is important to understand that if you want to figure out how to deal with your anger, you are going to need to find times of solitude; ten minutes, an hour, or an extended part of a day. It is difficult because we get so distracted by sights and sounds or by technology, or we think we might miss something like a television program or a news story or an important meeting. Jesus prioritized alone time so he could have his mind in the right place in order to do what God called him to do. We need that too.

Being alone may seem unnerving, daunting, or even scary. When we are faced with doing something we have never done or do not know how to do correctly, we tend to be dismissive. Solitude is more than about being alone. It is a way to clear your mind and bring clarity to the clutter of life, to bring understanding to the confusion of life, and to bring direction to the waywardness of life.

Confronting Issues

Jesus also confronted the issues that made him angry rather than to remain silent. He could have observed what was going on in the temple and just walked away. He could have written in his journal or written a strongly worded letter to the editor or to the high priest. He could have reasoned that anything he said or did would not make a difference because when he left, they went right back to what they were doing previously. Jesus did not bring immediate change to the temple. Jesus could have said to the Pharisees, I know you are wrong. You know you are wrong. Nothing is going to change so let's just go about our respective business." However, Jesus found it important to confront them and to confront the issues and injustices he witnessed.

Jesus did not confront every issue every day or argue with people constantly, but there are moments when Jesus says, "I can't keep silent anymore." For most of us, we think social convention demands that we do not tell people when we are angry. We do not want to tell people when they are wrong because it might hurt their feelings. We do not want to tell people when they are acting out in inappropriate ways because who am I to say they are wrong or being inappropriate? Jesus found it necessary to confront them. We need to learn how to say to people, "That type of behavior Is not going to work."

There are ways to confront issues and behaviors without being disrespectful or wreaking havoc. To begin, separate the person or persons involved from the behavior(s) and/issues that need confronted. The idea is to deal with what is wrong and why it is wrong rather than to express your anger, embarrass the person, or belittle the person. By showing respect for the person, you can diffuse the emotional tension.

Describe the offensive behavior as clearly as possible. General statements like "You always do this!" will not bring clarity to the situation. Identify the one action that needs addressed, give specific details, and be ready to provide examples of the behavior. This helps the person to understand that you are not just making things up, ranting because your feelings are hurt, or being authoritarian.

Next, explain how the behavior impacts you or others in a negative way. Again, there is a need to be as specific as possible. Tell who was hurt, how the behavior caused harm to a group or organization, or how the behavior causes other people harm or pain. People have a right to their opinions, but they do not have a right to hurt you or other people. By explaining the harm, you demonstrate the negative impact of the behavior.

Realize that people will not usually be receptive to your confrontation. They may argue with you, yell at you, be dismissive of you, or call you names. That kind of response is a defense mechanism kicking in. If and when that happens, maintain your calm, do not allow more harm, and if the other person gets violent, seek help immediately.

Finally, make sure you describe alternate behaviors that would be acceptable. Identifying the negative behavior is easy. Providing a positive alternative is not as easy. Make certain you are prepared with alternative behavior suggestions before confronting the offending party. Following these guidelines can help keep the monster at bay.

Accepting Personal Injustice

Another way Jesus managed his anger is that he accepted personal injustices. We get angry when we think justice has not worked in our favor or when we think we have been taken advantage of. We get mad because something happened that hurt us. Jesus did not get mad when people did things that hurt him. He got mad when people did things that hurt people he cared about. When injustice happened to Jesus, he accepted it. Do you think it was just that Jesus was nailed to a cross and executed for your behavior? Do you think he whined about it? Do you think he told God how unfair it was? Do you think he cried and pouted? Did he ask, "Why is life treating me like this?"

When personal injustice came to him, he absorbed it, he took it, he accepted it. He reasoned that if this is what he had to do to, what he had to bear to be the image of God to this creation, then he would endure the injustice. What Jesus would not bear was witnessing injustice spreading to other people.

We tend to be okay when injustice happens to other people. We are not okay when it happens to us. We spend little time or thought on the injustices that happen in our world, the things our country does that are unjust to people of other countries, or the mechanisms in place in our own communities that are unjust to the poor. Welfare keeps the poor impoverished. It was designed that way. We do not think anything of it. We do not speak out against it. We do not confront it. We invest almost nothing into caring about the injustices against the more and marginalized people of our town, of our state, of our country, of the world. We think if we spend more money on the problem (public and/or private funds) or give them more stuff (food, clothing, shelter) that it removes the injustice. We do not do anything about it. At best, we expect other to fight injustice on our behalf, whether it is a political group, a nonprofit organization, or a religious institution. We are wrong to think and act that way. Jesus accepted personal injustices, but he would not accept the injustices of his culture. He acted to resolve the injustice.

You and Anger

Here are three directions that can help us with our anger. We can see the differences between how the Bruce Banner and the Hulk managed anger compared to how Jesus managed anger. Jesus did not react in rage. These three directives can help you if you have anger issues.

First, recognize your triggers, know what makes you angry. Be aware of the things that make you angry. Sometimes we do not and, perhaps, will not know, but try to identify the cause of your anger. It may have nothing to do with the situation you are in. Maybe you are not getting enough rest.

53

Maybe you need to eat. Sometimes it could be that you are overwhelmed with all you have to manage at home or at your job. Maybe you feel powerless. Maybe you feel like you are being treated unjustly. If you do not recognize your triggers, you will never be able to manage your anger or stop unleashing the monster that rages within you.

Prayer and Meditation

Next, use prayer and meditation regularly. It is important to recognize the power of these tools to help you with your anger management. Admittedly, when you are in the middle of your anger or in a rage, you will not be able to stop and pray or meditate. Amid an escalating circumstance, you will not be able to pause and take a moment to pray, by that time it is too late. Even if you could, the person you are having a confrontation with would use it against you. They will use it to make you feel more powerless or to make you angrier.

What you need to do is use your prayer and meditation time before you get angry, to deal with those triggers, to release need to feel powerful, to let go of the need to be superior to everyone else, to release the need for the world to be just towards you, to rid yourself of the need to win or be right all of the time, and to emancipate the stress and stressors in your life. Use prayer and meditation for these purposes. It is not asking God to take your anger away, although that's how we usually pray. "God, help me to stop getting (being) angry." Instead, pray like this, "God, help me to recognize the things that bother (trigger) me. Help me not to be so selfish and self-absorbed. Help me to focus on the things that matter most in my world and not just me."

If you are just getting started with prayer and meditation, these steps may be helpful for you. It is beneficial to have a regular time to meditate and pray, but if you are schedule doesn't allow for that, be flexible and look for those moments you can get at least five minutes in solitude. Find a place where you will not be disturbed. Bedrooms, basements, closets, attics, barns, the woods, and cars can all be places of solitude. In your place of solitude, make sure you have a comfortable place to sit, a pillow, a stool, a chair, or on the floor with your back against the wall.

After you have decided on a location, silence all electronic devices. It might be best to put all electronics in another room. Distractions or the temptation to be distracting can make meditating difficult. Decide how long you want to practice and set a timer. I prefer to keep the timer in another room, so I am not tempted to glance at it repeatedly.

Next, close your eyes and take two or three deep breathes. After you inhale, hold your breath for a moment or two and slowly exhale. This helps your body to relax. Relax your shoulders, your arms, your legs, your hands, and your feet. Make sure you continue to sit upright with your back straight. As you continue breathing, relax your face (eyes, cheeks, brow). Focus your thoughts on your breathing. How does it feel when you inhale? How does it feel when you exhale? Follow your breath with your mind. Relax.

Now, try to silence your mind. You can count your breaths or count to a number as you inhale and then that same number as you exhale. It is common to get distracted. When you do, return to counting your breaths. If counting seems too mundane, find a word or phrase to repeat that helps you focus and relax. I am. I am enough. I am love. Life is good. Or, as an alternative, you can hum on your exhales and follow the resonating sound.

Finally, when the timer reminds you to finish your practice, take a deep cleansing breath and affirm yourself for the practice.

Remember, keep it simple. Meditation is not a task to cross off your list or a chore that demands your attention. It is a method of bringing calm to your life. Do not let it become a point of stress. Meditation is a practice to prepare you for the stresses of life. If you want to learn more about meditation, take to the internet and find many great teachings and practices to enhance your meditation.

Responding to Anger

Finally, respond rather than react. You know some people are good at pressing your buttons. Some of your children are better at it than others. You have a boss or a coworker who is good at messing with you to get you off your game, to make you frustrated and angry. If you know they can do it, prepare yourself ahead of time for when they try to do it.

How will you respond to them? Usually, you are not your best self when you react. Some people in some circumstances may do well reading a situation and reacting appropriately, but most people in most circumstances do not. You are much better when you have a planned response.

You know those times in your life when after a confrontation you think, "Why didn't I say/do this? Why did I say/do that? I wish I had said/done _____." The reason we do not say those things is because we are not prepared. We do not have planned responses, so we say the first thing that comes to mind, or we say nothing. Often, we feel humiliated. Or we just yell things that do not matter or are not even associated with the confrontation. Learn to respond rather than to react.

Whatever your issue is, whatever your trigger is, whatever it is that gets you angry, whether it is the news, government, your boss, your significant other, your children, your parents, your sibling(s), the bank, or something else, learn and practice a planned response to those triggers because they will happen over and over and over again until you can respond rather than react. Incrementally you will get better and managing your triggers and those things will not make you so angry.

Rage and anger have dominated our lives and they are everywhere in our culture. Many of us have spent years trying to get rid of or manage the anger we feel. We have seen the monster within and have felt the rage and power. Has anger controlled your life? Has it made you feel powerful or in control or superior? Have you damaged or hurt others with your anger? The Hulk, when he is angry, just destroys whatever is in his way. He does not think about the consequences. When we get angry, we usually bring destruction with us as well and seldom think about the consequences. It is time to find a better path.

Chapter 4: Thor: The Purpose of God and Religion

All of Moses' Teachings are summarized in a single statement, "Love your neighbor as you love yourself. (https://my.bible.com/bible/70/GAL.5.14)

How many religions do you think are in the world? According to www.ReligiousTolerance.org (http://www.religioustolerance.org/worldrel.htm), there are 19 major religions and about 270 sub-groups. Within Christianity, there are between 200 and 33,000 denomination or sects. It depends on who you ask and how they classify or define a denomination. When you look at the wiki page, you can see why it is so difficult to get a real grasp of the different groups (https://en.wikipedia.org/wiki/List_of_Christian_denominations). In addition to all of these groups, there are thousands of independent churches that have no denominational affiliation but could easily fit into one of the defined categories or groups.

These statistics remind us that there are thousands (if not tens of thousands) of ways to approach religion, G(g)od, and/or Christianity. The idea that one church, one movement, one denomination has it all right seems implausible. Rather than trying to explain how everyone else is wrong, perhaps a better approach is to see what we can learn from someone else's perspective and belief system.

Beginnings

This leads us to Asgard, home of the Norse gods. In the pantheon of Norse mythology, there are dozens of gods, goddesses, demi-gods, celestial or eternal beings, and countless characters and creatures in the nearly fifty realms of the Norse world. Most notably among them are Odin, king of the gods; Frigga, mother of the gods; Fjorgyn, mother of Thor and mistress of Odin; Loki, god of mischief; Thor, god of fertility, sky, and thunder; the Valkyries; Hel, ruler of the realm of the dead; and Aegir, god of the sea. The characters in these mythological tales all play a role in understanding the world we live in. The people who gathered and shared these stories lived more than fifteen hundred years ago, but eventually came to be known as Vikings.

The Vikings were explorers of their world, conquerors of their challengers, and sea travelling raiders who lived near the end of the eighth century CE until the end of the eleventh century. For them, life was an adventure with all the ugliness and beauty of life. For them, the world was enchanted, powerful, and directed by things (beings) beyond their control. The goal of life was not to avoid the struggles and reach a nirvana or heaven, but rather a way to show one's worth or value through doing great deeds that benefited both self and community (see https://norse-mythology.org/ for more information).

Thor

The Vikings gave us the Norse myths and legends that shaped the creation of Marvel's version of The Mighty Thor. In this saga, Odin sends his son, Thor, to earth to teach him humility. Odin blocks Thor's memories of his godhood, and puts Thor into the body of medical student, Donald Blake. Blake is partially disabled, but very virtuous. Years later, Blake, now a physician, goes to Norway for a vacation. While there, he witnesses aliens landing nearby. Instinctively, he hides in a cave where he finds a walking stick. Upon striking the stick against a rock, Blake is transformed into the mighty Thor, god of thunder.

This leads me to ask, what can we learn from the story of Thor? For every manner of thinking, for every train of thought, for every philosophical point of view, there is a purpose behind it. Our job is to find those purposes, or in a particular instance, that particular purpose. As mentioned previously, the Norse mythologies were told for the purpose of inspiring people to great adventures and noble deeds that made their world a better place to live in. How does Christianity compare with Norse mythology? Who wins the battle of philosophies between Thor and Jesus?

To answer this question, we must first ask another question. What is the purpose of Christianity? Maybe it is to get humans to heaven (nirvana). Maybe it is to get humanity and God into a better relationship, to repair humanity's broken nature and restore humanity's perfection so humans and God can exist in the same space. Or, maybe the question is too specific. More broadly, what is the purpose of religion in the world?

The Purpose of Religions

Let's look at three main purposes of religions in general. First, there is the quest for power and perfection. Religious leaders and institutions want power over their followers and control their behaviors. On the beneficent end there is the need to maintain order and civility. Religion helps provide a framework for that. Religion can define good and bad, provide structure for social mores, and help people figure out their place in the world. On the maleficent side, religion can oppress people or groups of people, justify violence towards people who believe differently, and prevent people from pursuing a path not approved by the religion.

Does this exist in Christianity? Yes, it absolutely does! The church wants power; power to control what people do and do not do, power to tell people how much of their money they should give to the church, power to tell people how they must behave or what they must believe to get to heaven or to avoid hell. Controlling other peoples' behavior in pursuit of perfection, either in this life or the next, is a purpose of religion.

There is also a quest for perfection. This quest leads to a moral code, written or unwritten, that describes best practices (behaviors) to instill in your life and worst practices (behaviors) to avoid in your life. Christians tend to believe that they have the best or highest moral code on the planet and throughout history. This is not true, but we like to believe it is. Other moral codes are stricter than Christianity's. For example, the moral code of Ancient Egypt was far more conservative than modern Christianity. Moses would have been brought up in this strict way of life and when he receives the ten commandments, they are strict, but not as confining as what he knew as an Egyptian. However, the need for perfection remained.

A second purpose of religion is unity and/or harmony. Unison would be if we were all singing the same notes of the same song in the same key and always on pitch. Harmony is when we sing the same song, but different singers sing different notes or tones of a musical scale that still sounds good together. Religions want people to believe the same way. We think that if we believe something and it has been helpful in our lives, then it would be good for other people to believe it as well because it could be helpful in their lives. There is a need for a unifying belief system.

At worst, we want a harmonizing belief system where we all hold the same basic beliefs, but some may believe something slightly different but harmonizing rather than dissonant. This creates a fuller theological sound and allows more people to find a pitch that fits their range and ability. Is there any of this in Christianity? Of course there is.

The stories may change slightly but the meaning behind the stories stays the same. Christianity in all its forms wants people to believe the same things. We compose and recite confessions of faith (or statements of faith), write anthologies of systematic theologies or practical theologies, band together with others to declare what is orthodox (correct beliefs) and what is unorthodox (incorrect beliefs), and to define orthopraxy (right practice) and non-orthopraxy (wrong practice). In our quest for unity, the church defines who is in and who is out, who goes to heaven and who does not, who is Christian and who is not.

One Christian creed is called the Apostle's Creed. Although not written by the apostles, it has been a part of the unification principle of Christianity from the middle of the second century CE. Here is the most common version:

I believe in God the Father Almighty, Maker of heaven and earth, And in Jesus Christ his only Son our Lord, Who was conceived by the Holy Ghost, Born of the Virgin Mary, Suffered under Pontius Pilate, Was crucified, dead, and buried. He descended into hell; The third day He rose again from the dead; He ascended into heaven, And sits on the right hand of God the Father Almighty; From thence he shall come to judge the quick and the dead. I believe in the Holy Ghost; The Holy catholic Church, the Communion of Saints; The Forgiveness of sins; The Resurrection of the body, And the Life everlasting. Amen.

If a Christian or a Christian organization diverges from just one of these points, they are considered unorthodox at best and heretical at worst. There is a need among Christians, theologians, Christian educators, and church leaders to make sure there is unity throughout Christianity. Christians only want to be with Christians who believe the same things. We gather in buildings and under signs that declare what we believe (Catholic, Baptist, Assemblies of God, Presbyterian, Lutheran, Brethren, Episcopalian, Anglican, etc.). These signs suggest what the people who attend believe and if you believe something else, you would be better to find a different church. After all, most people in most churches do not like it when people challenge or question their church's theology.

The third thing that religions look for or attempt to accomplish is the quest for understanding and self-fulfillment. May religions have as their purpose to understand the world we live in, how we got here, how we interact with (or should interact with) it, and humanity's role in this world. No doubt you have heard these ideas before. We want to know what is going on in our world. This is our quest for understanding and self-fulfillment. It is this quest that will reveal the next life or the afterlife.

We want something good for us after we die. We want something fulfilling in this life *and* something gratifying in the next life. This is the quest for the purpose of life and the rewards (or punishments) available to us in the afterlife. Christians speak of this quest in terms of heaven and hell. Other religions may speak of it as reincarnation. After you die, you get reborn as another person or creature to learn more about this life and gain higher understanding until eventually you reach nirvana or oneness with the one source of power in the universe.

Christianity and Christian churches push people to learn the Bible, to read more, to pray more, to experience more in hopes that these activities will bring the Christian closer to oneness with God, with God's will or purpose, or closer to sinless perfection or holiness. We want to know that our life in this world matters for the next world and for eternity.

Jesus

So, what makes Jesus different? What makes Jesus special? Why does the Gospel of John matter? What does Jesus bring to the table that other religions did not address? Why should anyone give Jesus more time and attention than they would give to Thor? Is life only about adventure, showing one's worth through noble acts and great victories over our enemies?

Here is what you need to know: if you are following Jesus because in so doing you will get to heaven; you have misunderstood the Gospel. You have misunderstood Jesus. It is not that getting to heaven is a bad thing. Quite the contrary. But, getting to heaven is not the purpose for following Jesus, it is a gift because you follow Jesus. It is not the reason to follow Jesus.

Jesus came to teach us three things. First, Jesus wanted an end to laws as a motivation for moral choice. He wanted to end the Law as the reason for doing one thing or avoiding doing another thing. Begin to think about the religions you know or the churches you are familiar with. Are there rules and laws that told followers what choices to make, which behaviors that are acceptable, and which behaviors are not acceptable?

If you have lived at all, you have lived with laws. You have them at work. You have them in school. You have them in society. You have them in church. Some of the laws or rules are written down, some are codified, others are not. There are unwritten rules and "bro codes" that govern our behavior to help us make moral choices.

Jesus taught that we should stop doing that. He taught that we should stop looking to the Law and stop looking to rules for reasons to make moral choices. Those are not good enough. But do we not still use them? Do we not use laws and rules and threats of punishment if you break those laws as a basis for making right choices? Do we not, as parents, do the same thing? We set rules and set consequences if those rules are broken. Is this not true everywhere in life? Jesus taught that his followers should think differently.

Jesus elevates above the law, or Law. He did not come to replace an old set of laws with a new set of laws. Rather, he came to transcend the law, to elevate our thinking and perspectives beyond the law; toward something better than law.

The principle Jesus said his followers should use when making moral choices is loving your neighbor. If I loved the person or the people with whom I was interacting, then how should I react in a given situation? If I wanted to communicate to those people that I love them, which words would I choose, what inflection or tone of voice would I use?

How would I treat my family if I wanted them to know I love them? How would I teach and correct my children if I wanted them to know I love them? How would I interact with government officials if I wanted those people to know that I loved them and cared about them?

These questions should create a powerful, rising impetus within us, compelling us to rise above the law. The law limits what we can or cannot do. Love rises above those limits. Laws define the least and/or most that is required of someone; a limit to how fast we can drive without encountering consequences, the least amount of money we must give to the government, how high I can let my grass grow, etc. Every law, every rule, every regulation limits personal liberty, whether in political context, religious context, social context, family context, work context, or educational context. Jesus taught that if his followers will work on loving people, it will change the way they live and the way they make decisions as they retreat from a law based mentality toward a love based one.

Additionally, Jesus wanted an end to the separation between humanity and divinity. All religions have a gap between mortals and immortals, between humans and deities. Then they find a way to bridge that gap. What makes humans more godlike? What makes gods more human? How can the two groups merge? What happens if a deity procreates with a human, or a mortal with an immortal? How do humans make a connection with God? All these questions are part of the quest for religious understanding. The birth story of Jesus is not entirely dissimilar to the birth story of Hercules. Both were born to human women impregnated by an eternal, divine, all-powerful, father god. The human impetus to combine the divine with the ordinary is strong. Even Norse mythology uses this device to push the understanding of noble acts and adventurous living.

Christianity teaches that we can connect with God through prayer, meditation, scripture reading, or worship. Some churches use rituals like communion or baptism to connect with God. In John 3, the writer explains that God sent Jesus to bridge the gap. Jesus' purpose was to allow us to interact with God without an intermediary. We do not need a priest. We do not need someone to offer sacrifices for us. We can interact we God directly because God is with us in a divine presence wherever we go. We do not need to light candles. We do not need to chant mantras. We do not need to invoke God's presence through prayers or by singing songs. God's presence is with us here, at your house, at my house, at your place of employment, or wherever-- all at the same time. Jesus came to give us access to God at all times.

The other thing Jesus came to do was to establish the primary principle of life. Jesus taught that what matters more than anything else is that we love people. When Jesus was asked what the greatest commandment is (or the greatest law), he said that the first is to love God and the second is like the first, love your neighbor as you love yourself (see Mathew 19:16-22; Mark 10:17-22; Luke 18:18-23). This becomes the motivating principle for the rest of the New Testament.

Paul wrote it this way in Galatians chapter 5 (which was actually written before any of the gospel accounts),

All of Moses' Teachings are summarized in a single statement, "Love your neighbor as you love yourself. (https://my.bible.com/bible/70/GAL.5.14)

That is the pinnacle of all the law. If you can do this, you understand the rest of it. As a matter of fact, the rest will not matter to you. If you will live your life with this one principle in mind, that you must love people at all times, no matter how you feel, no matter your emotional state, no matter what your financial state is, no matter their skin color, no matter their wealth or lack thereof, then you will understand the great commandment. Your goal is to love people. Period. That is the principle that was initiated with Jesus.

When we read John 3:16:

God loved the world this way: He gave his only Son so that everyone who believes in him will not die but will have eternal life. (https://my.bible.com/bible/70/JHN.3.16),

we need to understand that it isn't about eternal life in heaven. It is eternal life that begins now and never ends. It was never in the mind of God or Jesus or even the New Testament writers that people should accept the teachings of Jesus (evangelicals might say "get saved") and just wait to get to heaven either through death or the return of Christ. Jesus taught that if you were going to follow him, your life had to change now. You need to give up the law and start living under the principle of love. This is the primary focus of all that you do.

This idea is so hard for us. Laws are so engrained in our world. Rules are so deep-rooted in us. It is difficult to change. But Jesus said to get rid of the laws and rules. Stop trying to obey your way to God. Stop concerning yourself with heaven and hell. Start right now in this love relationship, not just a relationship with God, but a relationship with other human beings. Interact with them, care for them, show them that you love them. That is how people will see Jesus. This is what Jesus came for.

The thing that other religions cannot do; the thing that Thor could not do; Jesus did. Jesus did not come to rescue you from your financial crisis, although there are financial blessings when you follow Jesus. He did not come to rescue you from your relationship needs, although Jesus can help you put bad relationships back on the right track. That was not his purpose for coming. His purpose was not to keep you safe while you are driving or travelling, even though we pray for that often. It is not that God does not want you to be safe, but that is not why we follow Jesus. Jesus came so that you could elevate your life, so that you could learn to love people better, so you would love people more deeply, so that through your love for them, people will recognize Jesus.

That is an amazing thing! The only way people will ever recognize God in this world is by you loving them. That is powerful! Your theology does not matter. Your ability to follow the law does not matter. You must love people all the time not just on Sundays, but every day, consistently, throughout your life. We must show them what love is about.

When Jesus said that those who love him must come to the light so that their deeds can be seen by people, what do you think he meant? Why do you think he would say that? So that you could get a pat on the back for being good? No, but so that through your deeds of love, people will see him and their lives might change and they too could begin loving people and loving God.

One last question. Why are you following Jesus? Are you really in it to love people? Is it to get to heaven or to help other people have a better life filled with love and loving actions? Jesus came to make one of these possible. I hope you choose love.

Chapter 5: Doctor Strange: The Power of Prayer and Magic

"When you pray, don't be like hypocrites. They like to stand in synagogues and on street corners to pray so that everyone can see them. I can guarantee this truth: That will be their only reward. When you pray, go to your room and close the door. Pray privately to your Father who is with you. Your Father sees what you do in private. He will reward you. "When you pray, don't ramble like heathens who think they'll be heard if they talk a lot. Don't be like them. Your Father knows what you need before you ask him.

https://my.bible.com/bible/70/MAT.6.5-8

Do you believe in magic? I am fascinated by good magicians. Even when I know they are performing an illusion or sleight of hand; I marvel at their skills and my inability to detect their deceit. Real magic is different. Casting spells, calling on unknown forces, and attempting to manipulate the laws of nature seems unbelievable to me, but not to everybody. Many people believe in magic or witchcraft or sorcery.

Magic is the (apparent) power to influence people or events by using supernatural forces. It is enchantment or conjuring. It is the art of using charms or rituals to get what you want, good or bad.

Do you believe in prayer? I am fascinated to listen to people who pray with confidence and conviction. They, apparently, can call into being those things which are not. They can manipulate people and circumstances to get what they want out of life. They call upon unseen spiritual powers to intervene on their behalf and bring about whatever it is they think should happen. It is strange how similar magic and prayer appear to be.

Doctor Strange

Dr. Stephen Strange first appears in the Marvel Universe in 1963 as a creation of Stan Lee and Steve Ditko in Strange Tales #110. Dr. Strange is a neurosurgeon, one of the best in the world. One night he has an automobile accident and severely injures his hands to the extent that he is told he will never be able to practice as a doctor again. Surgeons like Dr. Strange tend to think that they are special, and for good reason. They have a special set of skills. Strange has put his entire self-worth into his medical skill and surgical genius.

The good doctor's inability to practice neurosurgery sends him on a mission to find a cure for his frail hands or to find a surgeon who can restore the use of his hands. In pursuit of this cure, Strange spends all his amassed wealth and all the wealth of others that he could borrow. When he is at his lowest point of desperation, he sells his last possession of value to get a ticket to the far east to find the Ancient One who supposedly has a magical cure for his hands. All he wants to do is get back to neurosurgery and then his life will be complete again.

Stephen Strange goes off in search for this ancient one and finds him on top of a tall mountain. The old man indeed has great wisdom and is well-practiced in the magical arts. However, he has no respect for Dr. Strange because the doctor only wants to use magic to cure himself and then go back to living his pre-accident life. He has no intention of trying to make the world better because of this new magical power, except to go back to New York City and heal people through his surgical skills. However, it is really not about making his patients' lives better as much as it is about his own importance in the community, his reputation, and his large lifestyle. He is a very selfish person.

Because Strange has no money, he cannot get back to the United States, so he returns again and again to the ancient one pleading for assistance. On one such visit, the ancient one is attacked by Baron Mordo. Doctor Strange comes to the aid of the ancient one and for the first time in his adult life, he does something that isn't selfish. In that moment, the ancient one begins to see that Stephen Strange has within him the ability to be selfless, the ability to do good.

Strange believes that if he works with the ancient one long enough, the ancient one will heal him and he'll be able to operate again. That never happens. From 1963 to present, Doctor Strange never has had his hands healed. Instead, he learns the mystical arts and the wisdom of the ancient one and eventually becomes the Sorcerer Supreme, protector of Earth. Doctor Strange becomes the watchman for any magical or mystical evil that might come to Earth. If evil threatens, he must defend against it magically.

Failures

There are three failures in Stephen Strange's life that are important to the story. First, he can be aloof. He is not approachable nor is he particularly likable. Just because he has magical powers does not mean he has a great personality. He is not a mean person, he just does not particularly care for other people. Other people are not up to his standard. He thinks he is better than most other people, smarter than most other people, and more powerful than most other people. They just aren't him.

Secondly, Strange has a superiority complex. He is vain. He really likes himself. He thinks he is so good in every way. Every thought he has is brilliant. He is someone who would tell you that you are not good enough or that you are a bad parent or that you stink as a spouse. He does not care if he offends you with his rendition of the truth.

Finally, he can be manipulative. One of the things about practicing magic, is that the practitioner must manipulate energy or forces to make that energy or those forces do what he needs it to do. Doctor Strange has difficulty realizing when he is manipulating people. Because he thinks he is smarter than everyone else, he thinks he can make you see things his way and will coerce you if necessary.

Magic

Magic has at least three purposes in our world. It provides practitioners with a sense of power and a sense of control, even if it is a false sense. It is the power to manipulate reality, usually by supernatural forces. Those who practice magic try to use things of the natural realm and manipulate them to bring about the world that they want. Magic is a way to create the reality that you want through spells, incantations, or conjuring.

Magic practitioners believe that magic can change the circumstances of their life or your life. They want to fix something that is wrong in their life or the life of someone they love. They believe circumstances can be changed by mixing the right herbs together or chanting a spell or creating a potion. Maybe they want to bring healing when they are sick, to help someone fall in love, to bring financial gain, or to bring hope. This is part of the practice of magic.

The third thing magic attempts to do, is to influence supernatural powers. This one is a little tricky because not everyone who practices magic believes in supernatural powers or supernatural beings. Not everyone who believes in supernatural powers or supernatural beings believes in magic. The ones who do believe in both supernatural powers and supernatural beings, think that those powers or beings can be harnessed or controlled using spells, charms, or incantations. Using magic, you can get supernatural beings to do your bidding or to help you accomplish your tasks.

As odd as many people think this is, all these things are what Christians use prayer to do. Those who believe in and practice magic, use its ritual and customs to help them get healthy, stay healthy, get wealthy, find jobs, find love, and ask unseen forces to intervene on their behalf. Christians pray that God will heal them, keep them healthy, provide for their financial need, help them find a job, help them find a life mate, and use spiritual forces or entities to keep them from harm. Perhaps magic is as strange to us as prayer is to non-religious or non-Christian people.

Jesus

"This is how you should pray: Our Father in heaven, let your name be kept holy. Let your kingdom come. Let your will be done on earth as it is done in heaven. Give us our daily bread today. Forgive us as we forgive others. Don't allow us to be tempted. Instead, rescue us from the evil one."

https://my.bible.com/bible/70/MAT.6.9-13

In Matthew chapter 6, Jesus teaches at least four things concerning prayer. There may be more, but I'll stay with these four. First, Jesus says we should pray that the kingdom, his kingdom, needs to become evident. When he says, "Pray like this…Your kingdom come and your will be done" (6:10), Jesus wants his followers to know that the new kingdom needs to become the new way of following God. While there is not time here to study the entire Gospel of Matthew, it is important for us to understand what that new kingdom is.

What is the kingdom of God? It is not heaven. Jesus is not telling his followers to pray that heaven comes to earth. The Sermon on the Mount, Matthew 5-7, is the primer to the new kingdom. Jesus is saying that his followers should pray that the new kingdom breaks into the world and becomes evident to people.

In Stephen Strange's world, the Marvel Universe, the doctor realizes that there are multiple dimensions and different worlds. Most people in any of the worlds have difficulty understanding that. People of Earth are no different. Doctor Strange must discern which beings from other realms can come into his world and which ones he must prevent. Strange understands that not everything is good and not everything will make things better.

How does that happen? What would it look like in our world? According to Matthew, Jesus wants his followers to pray that his kingdom becomes evident to others. For that to happen his followers must take the teachings of the new kingdom and teach them to people they know. Today, that can only happen through Christians. For you to participate in this new kingdom teaching, you need to be able understand it.

Explaining the kingdom of God can be complicated or we can simplify it so everyone can understand it. Churches and religious organizations like it complicated. Preachers and professors like it complicated. Regular followers of Jesus like it simple. The kingdom of God according to Jesus is simple, it is to love people. If you want people to know Jesus' kingdom, love them. Loving people is simple. Loving people is difficult.

How do we love people who, like Stephen Strange, think they are better than us? How do we love people who sell drugs to our kids? How do we love people involved in human trafficking? How do we love people who want to kill us? How do we love people who are doing evil and vile things so that the kingdom of Jesus is evident to them? That is more than difficult, right? It is nearly impossible.

Jesus says that we should pray that God's kingdom is evident to everyone. I doubt any of us have prayed that God's kingdom would be made known through us and the way we love others. If that were our daily prayer, that God's kingdom would become evident because of me, it might change how we behave towards others.

The second thing Jesus wants his followers to pray for is that they would have their daily bread today. That seems redundant. "Give us each day our daily bread" (v 11). Provide what we need today. While many around the world do not have the abundance we have here in the United States, most American Christians have more than enough for today, for this week, and possibly for this month.

Most American Christians do not pray that God will supply their daily need because we have more than enough for today. So, what would happen if that became our daily prayer? Instead of asking God to bless the food and make us strong and keep us healthy, maybe we could use the abundant resources we have to be the answer to someone else's prayer by helping to provide their daily need. How can we be less obsessed about our food and more concerned with how we can improve the lives of those who live among us. What if we did not store up weeks of food? Could we simply pray for our daily needs so that God's kingdom would become evident among the people with whom I come in contact.

Third, Jesus reminds his followers to make sure they pray for forgiveness. The caveat is that the prayer is that God will only forgive me as much as I forgive others. If I hold a grudge, I am praying that God will hold a grudge against me. Stephen Strange held a grudge against the driver who caused the accident that ruined his life. The ancient one, in return, held a grudge against Strange because of Strange's narcissism. Do you hold grudges? Can you hold grudges as you pray for God's kingdom to become evident?

Some of us carry hurts, anger, or bitterness for years. We cannot seem to forgive those who have spoiled our life plan, those who have caused accidents, and those who have entered our lives to bring pain and destruction. Forgiveness is difficult sometimes. When we find ourselves there, we have to wonder whether we are making God's kingdom evident, or making it look petty, judgmental, and foolish.

Jesus is not teaching that God will not forgive us. Rather, he is teaching that when we ask for something we are not willing to give, we are not understanding the new kingdom. When we want for ourselves what we cannot or will not give to others, God's kingdom will not be evident.

If you want God's kingdom to become evident in your world, what you have to do is to understand that all of the people who have wrecked your life need to see the new kingdom. It needs to become evident to them like it is evident to you. If it means that the only way for it to become evident is for you to love them, even though they hurt you, then you should choose to love them.

This does not mean you have to trust them or allow them space in your life where they can hurt you again. It simply means that you should let go of the grudge, the bitterness, the anger and replace it with a genuine love that wants the best for them.

It is hard.

Is it any wonder Jesus said we should pray like this every day?

Finally, Jesus teaches that his followers need to resist temptation. Why resist temptation? After all, didn't Jesus already provide forgiveness for sins? As long as you forgive others who do not resist temptation, God will forgive you for not resisting temptation. What does resisting temptation have to do with the kingdom Jesus is introducing?

If you want God's kingdom to be evident in your world, you need to resist temptation, the temptation to be selfish, the temptation to be aloof or separate from other people, and the temptation to be vain and to think that you are better than, holier than other people. These are temptations that separate you from other people, not from God. Jesus isn't suggesting that we need divine intervention so that we do not commit murder or steal from our neighbors.

Most people are not wicked and vile. As Jesus teaches his followers, he is not accusing them of being violent or prone to heinous acts. Our sins are not the things that separate us from God, they are the things that separate us from one another. It is our own self-interests, above all else, that is sinful. We need to resist the urge to be self-centered. The temptation, like Stephen Strange faced, to think that you are more special than other people, more righteous, more clever. The temptation to think you matter more than other people, your life is more important than other lives, and that your thoughts are higher than other peoples' thoughts is where we need help.

We prefer to pray for God's blessing on us and our loved ones (friends and family) but seldom give a thought about God's blessing on others. We want God's favor, even if it is at the expense of others. Doctor Strange wanted to perform surgeries because it made him feel good about himself. It made him feel important. He gave no thought to the idea that he could be a better help to more people if he would let go of his selfishness and serve the good of the world. One act of selflessness led him to a path that changed how he saw the world. He saw a new kingdom.

We want our hands fixed so we can go back to the life that we love. We want our emotional damage healed so we can have the life that we dream of living. We want our financial damage fixed so we can have the "stuff" that we want. If someone must go without so I can have another phone or car or television or pair of shoes, so what! That is the temptation that you and I cannot resist. That is why we need to pray to resist it.

Doctor Strange spends the rest of his life (from 1963 to present) unlearning his selfish ways. Regardless of the writer or the artist, the temptation to be self-centered, aloof, vain, uncaring, and unloving follows him. We are like that. We want what we want because it benefits us. When we do not get what we want, we are upset because all we really want is a blessing for us.

But the kingdom of God is not about you. The kingdom Jesus is revealing is not about you gathering all the blessing you can get. It is about you learning to bring love to people, to all people, so they can see who Jesus is. Jesus' kingdom is not about getting to heaven or getting your "Get Out of Hell FREE!" card. It is all about sharing Jesus in your community in a way that makes a difference in the way that they live. It is designed for us to meet the needs of others as much as meeting our own needs.

For most Christians, when we pray (if we pray), it is usually about changing our life circumstances or the circumstances of someone we care for. "God, I'm sick. Will you change that for me?" "God, I'm lonely. Will you change that for me?" Magically or spiritually, what is the difference? We simply want what we want because it will make our lives easier or better. If I pray and tag my prayer #InJesusName, then it will happen as I want. Magic words, incantations, call it whatever you want, we think it makes a difference.

We are wrong.

We ask God to provide us with a bigger home or a nicer car or a better paying job. We ask God to change our reality. Meanwhile, down the street, a child is being beaten by a parent and you could not care less about his reality. If only God would make your life easier. If only God would provide you with more, magically. It is all magic. Every prayer that we pray is "God, do magically what I cannot do for myself." Use the word "spiritually" if it makes you feel better, but the reality is the same.

That is not at all how Jesus taught us to pray.

Magic is about manipulating nature or the supernatural so you can get what you want. It is inherently self-focused.

Praying is not about unleashing spiritual forces to work on your behalf. It is about reminding yourself every day how you should live. It is inherently self-motivating so we can become better at focusing on others.

Can you become a better prayer practitioner? Can you look at the Lord's Prayer differently? Maybe you could pray these four things every day:

1. God, will you allow your kingdom to be evident, through me, to the people with whom I interact today.
2. God, will you help me to focus on the things that I need for today so that your kingdom will become evident to the people around me.

3. God, will you help me to resist the temptation to be aloof from people, to stand away from people who offend me, to turn my back on those who make me sick, and to think that I am better than the people I interact with today.
4. God, will you help me to offer forgiveness to people in the same way I receive your forgiveness so that your kingdom will be evident to them.

This is a powerful way to live. Try it and see if it opens your life to new realities.

Chapter 6: Ghost Rider: Vengeance is Mine!

"Stop judging so that you will not be judged. Otherwise, you will be judged by the same standard you use to judge others. The standards you use for others will be applied to you. So why do you see the piece of sawdust in another believer's eye and not notice the wooden beam in your own eye? How can you say to another believer, 'Let me take the piece of sawdust out of your eye,' when you have a beam in your own eye? You hypocrite! First remove the beam from your own eye. Then you will see clearly to remove the piece of sawdust from another believer's eye. (https://my.bible.com/bible/70/MAT.7.1-5)*

Revenge is a human instinct. Wanting revenge is a normal part of existence. It is the desire to exact pain on someone, or some group of people, who has hurt me or someone I love (or you or someone you love). It is a dangerous thing.

Have you ever wanted revenge? Has there been a time in your life when you wished for someone to feel pain because of the pain they have caused? Most of us have had that sensation. It is something that has been around since the beginning of humanity. Ghost Rider and Jesus approach judgment and revenge from very different angles. Who do you identify with the most?

Ghost Rider

Ghost Rider has his beginnings back in 1973 when Roy Thomas created the character and Mike Ploog was the artist in the first issue. Ghost Rider is the story of Johnny Blaze, a stunt motorcycle rider. He's the son of Barton Blaze and Naomi Kale, carnival performers.

Johnny spends his life entertaining people with his motorcycle theatrics. While he was young, Johnny's dad was killed in a stunt that went sideways. In the aftermath, Naomi takes Johnny's younger brother but leaves Johnny as she runs away to find a better life for herself. Johnny is left with the carnival folks and is adopted by another carnival family.

Johnny has many anxious and angry feelings about the death of his father, thinking it was unfair. As a way of coping with these feelings, he begins dabbling in the occult. One day, while soothing his anger using occult practices, a figure, claiming to be the devil, appears to him and offers to help Johnny. At first, Johnny wants nothing to do with the devil or the deal, but his stepfather is almost immediately diagnosed with terminal cancer, so he reconsiders the offer.

The demon claiming to be the devil is actually Mephisto who tells Johnny that his stepfather can be healed from his cancer if Johnny will give his soul to Mephisto. After long hours of deliberation, Johnny reluctantly agrees and sacrifices his soul for the life of his stepfather. Mephisto is true to his word and Johnny's stepfather is healed from cancer but dies shortly thereafter in a motorcycle stunt that goes awry.

Johnny is furious with Mephisto for taking his stepfathers life, and so, as a way to make it up to Johnny, Mephisto gives Johnny the power to judge the souls of other people and to exact revenge on them if they have done anything wrong. In return, Mephisto will get all the souls of all the people that Johnny, as Ghost Rider, will judge. These souls will empower Mephisto and provide Johnny with a sense of justice.

Mephisto gives Johnny Blaze the power to judge the motives, intents, and character of the people with whom he comes in contact. When those people are judged to be evil, he turns into the Ghost Rider and exacts revenge for the evil they've caused, often killing them. It becomes an interesting thing to have the power to judge not only the actions of a person, but that person's intents and motives as well as their character.

Johnny Blaze has this ability because he is possessed by the power of the demon, Mephisto. He can *rightly* judge the character and content of other people's souls. Judgment leads to vengeance. Humans like the idea of judging the character and motives and intents of other humans. How does this idea compare to what Jesus taught?

Jesus

In Jesus day, Jewish people followed the Law. Roman law mattered to them, but not to the extent of Jewish Law, the

Pentateuch and the Talmud. People were judged according to how well they kept the laws. Sometimes judgment came in the natural world and sometimes in the afterlife. Everyone will be judged by the Jewish Law and the Jewish Law is final. Rabbis had final say on how to interpret and apply the Jewish Law.

In the Old Testament Law, there is a passage that states "an eye for an eye" (Leviticus 24:20, Exodus 21:24, Deuteronomy 19:21) suggesting that if one person harms another person, fair judgment is to have that same harm done to the offender. It was a way of exacting revenge without it getting out of hand. So, if someone damaged your eye, you have the right to damage their eye, but not both of their eyes. If someone killed one of your cows, you had the right to kill one of their cows as fair revenge, but you did not have the right to kill all their cows. A cow for a cow or an eye for an eye. An equal payment for the pain or loss you have suffered.

This idea is still around today. We see it often as a justification for war, violence, or neighbor disputes. Many wars are between two groups of people who believe they have been wronged in some way and that group wants to exact pain and suffering on the group of people they believe are responsible for their pain and suffering. This can go on for generations with both sides claiming to be exacting revenge or dispensing justice.

Ghost Rider only appears when evil is present and so most people are afraid of him when they see him because they fear his judgment. Jesus and the Old Testament Law often bring out the fear in people because they think God, Jesus, the church, or the members of a church are going to judge them.

This is a fair criticism of the 21st century Christian church. Unchurched people, and churched people too, if we are being completely forthright, often fear the judgments of other people in the church. We are afraid people will judge us by the way we dress, the way we talk, the way we live, the way we think, or any number of things.

To understand Jesus, we need to wrestle with this passage in Matthew 7. Here Jesus teaches that his followers need to release all judgments. Stop judging people entirely. He says his followers should not judge at all. The reason for that is that it is not for people to exact revenge on people. The job of followers of Jesus is to love people. They are released from the burdensome duty of judging others. It is not their job to judge the content of somebody's character. It is not their job to judge another person's soul. It is not their job to judge someone else's behavior.

Jesus continues to say if his followers judge others, they will be judged in the same way. If they judge people by their words or by their behaviors, then they will be judged by their words or your behaviors. Jesus teaches his followers to set that kind of judgment aside.

Jesus also teaches that we need to be set free from the Law. Paul writes about this idea throughout his letters. He is very clear about that. People should not follow the Jewish Law (the Old Testament) anymore because the Jewish Law exacts punitive damage on those who transgress or break the Jewish Law. That is not who followers of Jesus are though. Jesus has a new kingdom with a new way of thinking and a new way of doing things. Remember, his new kingdom is free from the Law.

Where Ghost Rider has a supernatural strength that comes from a demon, Jesus has a supernatural strength that comes from God. He has the ability to endure. He has the ability, power, and strength to deliver on this promise that he has given his followers; that if they give up their desire for judgments, good things will happen for them.

Johnny is possessed by a demon in search of vengeance and power while Jesus is possessed by the power of love. What he is trying to explain is that the power of love can change people's lives and even their eternal fate. The power of Ghost Rider to alter people's lives was never a good thing for those being judged. Jesus can change the present state and the eternal fate of the people with whom he comes in contact through his followers, and it is always going to be good.

Johnny Blaze as Ghost Rider acts through the power of a demon to exact judgment and vengeance on people to get them to pay for the sins they have committed during their lives. Jesus acts through his followers in the power of love to love people regardless of the sins they may have committed so they can understand how love can change the world. That is a powerful message of hope as opposed to the message of fear from Ghost Rider.

Our Lives

You and I have been conditioned for law and order. Laws matter. We are a nation of laws; a nation of rules and we should follow those laws and rules as part of our civic duty. It is not necessarily bad to follow laws and rules, but not all rules and laws are created equal. All rules and laws are created by human beings and I think that is one reason Jesus says we need to be set free from the Law. We always should be free to act in a loving way without being compelled by or bound by some law or rule to motivate us to act lovingly. We should act lovingly because of who we are not because someone told us to or threatened us with punishment if we did not.

We have been inured for law and justice. We have been taught from our youth for the need for laws and the need for justice. Justice must be served. We talk about restorative justice, that is, rehabilitating the offender rather than punishing the offender. We talk about retributive justice, that is punishing the offender swiftly and fairly. We talk about distributive justice, that is making sure costs, resources, and justice itself are distributed equally and equitably throughout the population. We even talk about redistributive justice, that is, paying people back for legal or social injustices done to a person or a person's ancestor.

These thoughts spring from a need for justice and/or a need for revenge or vengeance upon those who have acted unjustly. None of these ideas about law and justice come from a primary philosophy of love. People who want to exact revenge on another are not doing it out of love. They do it out of fear or hatred or greed or a sense of injustice. Or, they are doing it from a sense of pain they have felt or someone they love has felt and they want someone else to feel that pain as a form of justice for the wrong that caused the initial pain.

People may talk about what is fair when discussing law and justice. Fairness is a subjective word that can never really balance any scale. When people are demanding fairness, they are not demanding it out of a sense of love for others, but out of a sense of injustice (or possible injustice), a sense of pain (perceived or real), or a sense of revenge.

Our Powers

Our power as followers of Jesus is this, self-judgment. I should judge me. You should judge you. Jesus says, why do you mention the speck of sawdust in one person's eye when you have an entire log sticking out of yours! (Matthew 7:3) While this is a way for the writer to be humorous, it illustrates a meaningful point. What Jesus is telling us is that his followers should be self-reflective. Jesus' followers should focus on their own faults and shortcomings rather than the faults and shortcomings of others.

What part of my life am I not as loving as I need to be? Am I becoming more vengeful? How am I pointing out other people's flaws when I have so many of my own? Why am I concerned with a minor detail in someone else's life when I have so many things wrong in my own life? For many of us, being self-reflective is difficult, but it is what Jesus is teaching here.

Another aspect of this power is to be reflective of our own spirituality, our own behavior, and our own thoughts. We need to perform a self-critique. Ghost Rider performs a critique on other people, judging their thoughts, motives, intents, behaviors, and character. After he judges a person, he punishes that person immediately. We are not supposed to do that to other people, but we should be doing it to ourselves regularly. We do not need just to be self-reflective. We need to be critical of our own words, actions, motives, and character. Maybe I did not love that person the way that I should have. Maybe I did not say something in a way that communicates love. Maybe when I was frustrated, I used a tone of voice that did not reflect love. We all act in ways, speak in ways, think in ways, and live in ways, at some points in our lives, that are imperfect and unloving.

What happens with some of us is that as we are self-reflective, we become self-critical and then we want to punish ourselves for our imperfections, like Ghost Rider does to those he judges. When we get to the point where we want revenge on ourselves for what we have done wrong, we've forgotten that Jesus taught us to love ourselves. Martin Luther would flog himself for his imperfections or perceived sins. He would take a whip and crack his own back with it because he thought he was so sinful.

Self-punishment is not a part of following Jesus. For many people, this self-punishment may be verbal; vocal and/or internal dialogue reciting faults, calling names, or expressing extreme disgust. Other people use physical punishment by hitting or cutting themselves similar to what Martin Luther did. Too often, we think the pain we cause ourselves, mentally, emotionally, or physically, is justified because we are bad people or we have character, motives, intents, or behaviors that do not pass the self-judgment test. But we should not be punishing ourselves.

Jesus said we should love our neighbors the way we love ourselves. If we are not able to love ourselves, even in our flaws, we will not be able to love others in their flaws. Although some feel guilty about loving self because it feels selfish, vain, or conceited, it is necessary for to overcome the urge to self-punish.

Another of our superpowers is the power to forgive. This requires self-forgiveness. Sometimes we just have to say, "I am not a perfect human being. I will never be a perfect human being." Sometimes I blow it. Sometimes I am not nice when I should be. Sometimes I am not there when someone needs me. I am not always welcoming when I should be. I can get frustrated with myself when I have opportunities to show love to people, whether they are church folks or people in the community, and I just check out; I am not interested. This happens because I am in "self" mode not "loving" mode. Often, it is difficult to forgive myself. I will beat myself up over it and I will hate myself for it for a couple of days. Eventually, my superpower kicks in I learn that judgment is not the way forward.

You have the power of self-forgiveness too. Sometimes we need to just look in a mirror and say, "I forgive you" to the person looking back. It is okay to not be perfect or to be imperfect. Keep trying. Keep doing better. Keep asking for help. Eventually, you will be better at loving people. You will be better at understanding and loving yourself. You will get better at not wanting revenge. You will get better at not judging people. You will get better at loving yourself. You will get better at forgiving.

Remember, Johnny Blaze was possessed by the power of a demon, but you are possessed by the power of love. I want you to know that you are possessed by the love of God. The love of God dwells in you richly. That is a tremendous power.

Johnny Blaze did not act on his own. He did not get to choose who to judge. It was the power of the demon that came alive in him that caused him to pass judgment. With the power of love in our lives, the power of the love of God in our lives, we have the opportunity to allow God to come alive in us in those moments when we have opportunity to love people. We can show them a better way and give them a different way of looking at the world than they have ever had. We can give them a different way to see the church than they have known.

It is this power of the love of God in your life that can change the world. If you can release the power of love, rather than the power of judgment or vengeance, into your community, into your family, into your school, into your co-workers, you can change their worlds! You can let them know that have an opportunity to join a community that has forsaken judgment and embraced love. They can let go of fear and take hold of life.

Chapter 7: Ironman: Redemption

"Stop storing up treasures for yourselves on earth, where moths and rust destroy and thieves break in and steal. Instead, store up treasures for yourselves in heaven, where moths and rust don't destroy and thieves don't break in and steal. Your heart will be where your treasure is.
(https://my.bible.com/bible/70/MAT.6.19-21)

Most of us dream of being unimaginably wealthy. Story writers in books, plays, television, and movies often explore the lives of wealth-laden characters. There is something about that lifestyle that seems so exciting or glamourous or enticing. When the lead character is rich, charming, good looking, and a genius, it is irresistible!

Ironman

That brings us to Ironman. Created by Stan Lee in 1963, Ironman is a product of the Cold War culture. He first appears in Tales of Suspense #39. Jack Kirby did the art for the cover and Don Heck did the pages. Larry Lieber was the writer in the debut book. Ironman would not get his own book until 1968. In Tales of Suspense #48, the artist, Steve Ditko changes bulky grey armor to the red and golden armor we are so accustomed to seeing.

Tony Stark is the anti-communist, pro-capitalist, business magnate who becomes Ironman. Modeled after Howard Hughes (Tony's father is named Howard), Tony is a flamboyant adventurer, a lady's man, a millionaire (later a billionaire) and a genius. Tony is a pro war, pro munitions tycoon who inherits his father Howard's tech company and turns it into a weapons business. Stark Enterprises will sell weapons to anyone in the world willing to pay for them.

One day, Stark is injured in a booby trap and is subsequently captured by the enemy, the North Vietnamese army. He takes shrapnel to the chest and is danger of dying. While in captivity, he is connected with another prisoner who was a Nobel Prize winning physicist named Ho Yinsen. Yinsen and Stark create the gray armor Ironman and the magnetic plate that prevents the shrapnel from entering Stark's chest and killing him.

Stan Lee wanted a hero whose heart was literally and figuratively broken. Stark suffered the loss of his parents and now, potentially, the loss of is heart, his life. As Stark tries to escape the military prison camp while wearing the gray armor, Yinsen sacrifices his own life so Tony can get away. Stark escapes and goes back to his life as a playboy, business magnate. He struggles to come to terms with his own mortality and eventually tries to numb himself with alcohol and trivial relationships.

Stark is the quintessential pompous, self-absorbed, narcissistic man who is profiting from the death of other human beings. He profited from his father's death. He profited from Yinsen's death, and he profited from all the unnamed deaths from his weapons. How could this man be a hero? And

99

yet, he becomes one of the greatest hero's in the Marvel Universe.

Tony Stark values wealth, women, and weapons. He finds his self-worth in his incredible wealth and he flaunts it openly. He prides himself on his ability to seduce and control any woman he desires; no one says "no" to him. War and weapons are a part of human existence and Stark believes he has made it an art. Although there is nothing inherently wrong with wealth, women, or weapons, Tony uses these things simply for his own pleasure and gives no thought to how he is harming other people. He cares nothing about how he builds his wealth. He cares nothing about what happens to the women he is with after he discards them. He cares nothing about the weapons that he manufactures that kill or maim people and destroy homes, businesses, and property. He is totally self-absorbed. His treasure is all wrapped up in himself.

After coming to a realization that he needs to change his life, Tony tries to use Ironman to redeem his past failures. He doesn't stop doing the things that have made his life miserable, but he tries to do more good than bad. Tony may be a genius, but he struggles with depression. He may be millionaire or a billionaire, but he struggles with anxiety. He may be a playboy, but he suffers from loneliness. He may be a philanthropist, but he cannot do good to himself. He lives his life trying to redeem the bad choices he has made, but no matter how much good he does, he cannot shake the bad.

For many of us, we feel the guilt and pressure of the things we have done in the past that have hurt other people.

The church sometimes calls them sins. The secular world calls them mistakes or crimes. Maybe it something we said that hurts someone else. Maybe it is having the opportunity to help someone, but we turn a blind eye. Maybe we had a chance to intervene in a difficult situation but did not want to put ourselves at risk and then someone gets hurt (like Peter Parker with the thief). These things haunt us, and we replay them in our minds. We re-live these bad choices and bad moments in our lives while trying to figure out how to make it better, how to redeem our mistakes. That is the story of Tony Stark from 1963 until today.

Jesus

How does the story of Jesus compare with the story of Ironman? First, while Tony Stark grew up with a silver spoon in his mouth, Jesus would have grown up poor. Stark had all the luxuries of life while Jesus had very little. There are very few stories about Jesus as a child, and even fewer that made it into the Bible. One story is in Luke 2:21-24. Here, Joseph and Mary bring Jesus to the temple to offer a sacrifice to God for the birth of their son. They offer two turtledoves, the lowest offering allowed and the most they could afford. This speaks the poverty of the family into which Jesus was born.

Stark lives a life of notoriety, graduating from MIT at 15. Jesus was relatively unnoticed as a young man. He does not have followers or anyone to chronicle his life. He begins his ministry around age 30 and is crucified by the time is he 33. There are no known writings about Jesus for another twenty years or more. He lives an unimpressive, pedestrian, and financially poor life.

As far as the Bible records, and not much else exists about Jesus' life that is considered reliable, Jesus does not take a wife. We have no writings about his family life, his potential marriages, or his desire to have children, or his friends. While rumors persist in the church about Jesus and Mary Magdalene, there is nothing verifiable to conclude that they were a couple. Unlike Tony Stark, who was a womanizer, Jesus seems to be celibate, another remarkable contrast.

By the time Jesus begins his ministry, there is no mention of Joseph, his father, in the Biblical text. What happened to Joseph is unknown, but clearly Jesus' father is gone by the time Jesus is an adult. Mary, Jesus' mother is featured prominently in the Gospels. Like Stark, Jesus lives his adult life without a father. Unlike Stark, Jesus has a mother he interacts with throughout his adult life.

Jesus lives his life developing the idea of the new kingdom, a teaching that is different than the accepted views of God and religion. He spends his time and efforts teaching the primacy of loving other people. This is verified in the writings of Paul and in the Gospels. Jesus has no home. He does not own property. He does not work a job. He does not seem to have any possessions at all. It appears that Jesus has given up all that he had in service to other human beings. He lived off the generosity of others. This is as far from Tony Stark as you can get.

In the end, Jesus gives up his life to redeem the lives of other people, all other people. Compare that with Tony Stark. Stark tries to redeem his own life while caring little for the other people in the world. Yes, Ironman saves some people and rescues some from harm or even death. But he never changes the lives of those he saves. He never befriends them or offers to teach them how to protect or defend themselves. He never offers them an armor. He never tries to make their lives better after he rescues them.

The one person in the Ironman story, the one who plays the redeemer, is Yinsen, who sacrifices his life so Tony could live and hopefully change the world. Jesus lived his life for the benefit of others. Through his death, Jesus offers people a chance to learn a new way of living that will improve their lives. That story of redemption becomes the model that Paul and the Gospel writers use to teach people how to live and how to love.

You

Most of us were born in obscurity. The world did not take notice when we were born, when we went to school, when we graduated, or even our vocational choices. Most of us are not child prodigies, geniuses, or millionaires. With seven and a half billion people in the world today, it seems unlikely that anyone would notice any of us. We live our lives relatively unnoticed.

We search for accomplishment in our lives. Like Tony Stark, we want markers in our lives that say we matter. For some, it is a college education. For others, it is a business or a position at a job where we're recognized and appreciated. For some we take pride in our home or in our sense of fashion or in our financial portfolio or in athletics. We find things to treasure to help us know that our lives matter.

We love it when people tell us that we are good. We love accolades. We like giving and receiving awards. We appreciate, "Best Father Ever" t-shirts. A business leader once told me that the employees at his place of business loved receiving gold foil stars for the name tags because it showed that someone recognized their hard work and dedication. We have a need to be valued and we treasure the times when people value us.

There is an industry built around helping people live a more successful life with more money and more possessions. We can say, "Look at my house! I have done well!" or "Look at the car I drive! I'm so successful!" While there is nothing wrong with wealth, houses, cars, or possessions, these things do not necessarily speak to a life well lived. When we treasure these things and live our lives for these things, like Tony Stark did, you miss out on much of what makes life special, like Tony Stark did.

Alternatively, people have lived their lives in service to other people. They have cared for their spouse, their children, their parents, and their neighbors. Too often these servants get to the end of their lives and wonder if it was worth it. They will die unnoticed and mostly unappreciated. They, too, have missed out on what makes life special.

If you are like me and you have tried to love people and to serve people, however imperfectly, you quickly realize that people take advantage of you. They take you, your love for them, and your service to them for granted. They come to expect that you will serve them, that you will always love them. They do not return your graciousness. It does not make you feel valued or help you feel valuable because the world does not value that type of life. Rarely does someone like Mother Teresa, Saint of Calcutta, come around and gain notoriety because of a life of service.

The truth is that most of us would not attend a seminar that teaches how to do what Mother Teresa did. We will pay hundreds of dollars to figure out how to make more money, how to invest in real estate, how to build wealth, or how to be a better leader, but we would not spend a dime to figure out how we could better serve those in need around the world. We would not think about nursing the sick or housing the homeless and getting nothing for it. We do not value that if it is outside our family.

The teaching of Jesus in Matthew is clear. Followers of Jesus should treasure people over property or possession. Our mission is not to help people avoid hell or to gain heaven. What comes after this life will take care of itself. Our mission is to redeem the people in this world through the teachings of Jesus. Our job is to redeem other people, not ourselves.

Tony Stark lived his life trying to redeem his own life and never did it successfully. If he felt better about himself because he stopped a criminal or prevented mass destruction or even the death of hundreds, then that was good enough for him. As long as he felt good about himself, it was good. He has no real concern for the real needs of people in the world. And while he gave away millions of (fictional) dollars, he never brought change to the world.

We have people like that in our world today, people who give hundreds, thousands, or millions of dollars to businesses, government agencies, religious institutions, or nonprofit organizations. They give of their excess to get something back, even if what they get back is not monetary. They want to feel good about themselves. They want to be recognized for helping others, as a philanthropist. They want to gain notoriety for their philanthropy. They want to redeem their lives from the mistakes they have made or the people they have taken advantage of, or for their own failures and shortcomings. Maybe they just want a corporate advantage when they need a favor from a politician, or they want a tax break.

Our job, as followers of Jesus, is to redeem the people of the world. Our role is not to simply accept things as they are, but to help people see the teachings of Jesus in a light that will improve the way they live. We are not trying to change their eternal destination. We are trying to make a difference in the everyday lives of people. The teaching of Jesus is that if his followers would live sacrificially, give up of their own, live for the benefit of others, and constantly work to love people better, the world will become a better place.

Tony Stark believes in self-redemption through doing more good than bad. Jesus taught that through living sacrificially in the power of love, the world could be redeemed. We do not make ourselves better by doing more good in the world. We make the world better by learning to love and then teaching others to love.

Tony Stark, Ironman, does not care if people trying to bring harm to the world ever stop trying to bring harm to the world. He never has a conversation with a villain that gets the villain to stop doing evil in the world. He never invites the villain into a relationship to help the villain see a better way of living. He simply does not care.

Jesus never attacked or killed a single person. He lived his life trying to change the world. He taught people how to love, invited people into a relationship, and changed the lives of hundreds of millions of people. He treasured people and asks his followers to treasure people as well.

Chapter 8: The Black Panther: Ruler, Provider, and Protector

God saved us and called us to be holy, not because of what we had done, but because of his own plan and kindness. Before the world began, God planned that Christ Jesus would show us God's kindness. Now with the coming of our Savior Christ Jesus, he has revealed it. Christ has destroyed death, and through the Good News he has brought eternal life into full view. I was appointed to be a messenger of this Good News, an apostle, and a teacher. For this reason I suffer as I do. However, I'm not ashamed. I know whom I trust. I'm convinced that he is able to protect what he had entrusted to me until that day. With faith and love for Christ Jesus, consider what you heard me say to be the pattern of accurate teachings. With the help of the Holy Spirit who lives in us, protect the Good News that has been entrusted to you.

(https://my.bible.com/bible/70/2TI.1.9-14)

The American experiment was a specific way political thought progressed from the dark Ages into the Enlightenment and through the 20th century. Still, Americans have a fascination with kings, queens, princes, princesses, and royals in general. Disney has made a million fortunes telling girls that they are princesses. Bible passages, and thus Christians, talk about how God or Jesus is a king. The interest in kings and kingdoms seems to have no end.

In family systems, the traditional few was that men were the provider and protectors of the home while women were the caretakers and domestic engineers of the family. Much of that traditional thinking still exists in 21st century America. Bible passages, and thus Christians, seem to support this traditional view.

The Black Panther is a product of these traditional viewpoints, ruler, provider, protector. Many Christians view God or Jesus as ruler, provider, and protector as well. How are these two (Black Panther and Jesus) similar? How are they different? Is it possible that we misunderstand them both? Let's look at them and see.

The Black Panther

The Black Panther is a character created in 1966 by Stan Lee and Jack Kirby. His first appearance is in Avengers #52 and he does not get his own book until 1973. It took a long time for Marvel to give him a chance as a solo hero in *Jungle Action* and eventually a self-titled comic in 1977. His self-titled book was cancelled in 1979.

Stan Lee was the first to create an African superhero. There were other black characters appearing in comics at the time, but none were heroes. Marvel Comics broke the color barrier and introduced T'Challa, an African king and protector of the nation of Wakanda. While the Black Panther's name implies a connection to the political group by the same name, the hero is not overtly political, especially in the American political system.

T'Challa plays a dual role as leader of the nation and protector of the people and the wealth of Wakanda. As king, he inherits his power and authority from his father, but as a hero, he gets his superpowers from drinking the essence of a heart-shaped herb only grown in Wakanda. This herb gives him enhanced strength and speed, heightened stamina, agility, and durability, superhuman senses, rapid healing, and cat-like reflexes.

These special powers allow the Black Panther to fight intruders or other clan leaders who may want to overtake Wakanda or steal its resources. While there are others who can and do fight, the Black Panther is the unquestioned leader and the first line of defense.

As King of Wakanda and Chieftain of the Panther Clan, T'Challa is the guardian of the wealth and technology of Wakanda. What makes Wakanda special is that it is the only place in the world where you can find vibranium, a mineral stronger than any substance on earth (Captain America's shield is made from vibranium). Because of the scarcity of this mineral and the wealth Wakanda has amassed because of it, the nation has been kept hidden from the rest of the world. The people and leaders of Wakanda feared that other nations may invade their peaceful home or other people would get vibranium and use it for evil. Withdrawing from the world was their safest option.

T'Challa acts as an ambassador for Wakanda, attending political conferences and meeting with world leaders, but he never speaks a word about where his nation is or its vast wealth or its valuable resource. The other world leaders have no idea Wakanda is an advanced culture with tremendous technology and an excellent educational system. T'Challa is the ruler of a kingdom with resources to make the world a better place, but keeps those resources hidden.

Jesus

In the passage from 2 Timothy, Paul tells his readers that Jesus came to earth to demonstrate kindness. Most people have been taught that Jesus came to save the world or to forgive our sins. But Paul says that from the beginning, God chose Jesus to show the world his kindness. Of all the things that Jesus could have shown the world (the power of God, the wisdom of God, the creativeness of God, etc.), he is an ambassador of God's kindness.

Jesus is the destroyer of death, the creator of eternal life, and the exemplar of kindness. Of all the pictures we have of Jesus, we do not necessarily see Jesus as the destroyer of death. Paul is actually in prison waiting to die as he writes this letter. It is more than ironic that he chooses the destroyer of death as the moniker of Jesus. Paul wrote this letter somewhere in the mid 60's CE, during the reign of Nero. As far as I know, death did not end in the first century. Paul was familiar with death and so a literal interpretation of this seems absurd. We still have to face death. Paul is suggesting that physical death is not the end of life. Jesus demonstrates that. The most likely story of Jesus that Paul alludes to here is the resurrection. Paul obviously believes that there is something more after physical death. Jesus changed the idea that life is only physical, thus destroying the power of death.

In contrast to death, Jesus creates eternal life. Paul is, perhaps, suggesting that before Jesus, there was no eternal life for humans. At the very least, Paul thinks that because of the life, ministry, death, and resurrection of Jesus that humans can now have a fuller understanding of eternal life. It is the Good News that brings eternal life into full view. The Good News is not that Jesus lived, died, and resurrected. It is not that Jesus died on the cross for the sins of the world. The Good News is that people have been set free from the law and are now free to love people following the example of Jesus.

More than this, Paul says that Jesus gives us eternal life through his kindness, as opposed to because of our obedience, subjection, or faithfulness. Eternal life is not earned by praying a sinner's prayer, through following (obeying) the Law, showing piety, or doing acts of kindness. Jesus provides eternal life through his kindness. He is the example, the pattern for our lives to express kindness to others.

Jesus teaches about a new kingdom but in this kingdom, Jesus is not a king. He is not an empirical ruler making laws, judging disputes, or upholding the law (Law). Isaiah refers to the messiah as the prince of peace and there are numerous other texts in the Bible referencing God as king. Nathaniel calls Jesus a king. The Romans mock Jesus by calling him King of the Jews as they crucify him. Revelation has many verses about Jesus or the Lamb sitting on a throne.

There are other passages that suggest Jesus rules over the kings of the earth. However, Jesus is not a king in the dynastic or monarchial sense. Rather, he is an ambassador of God's kingdom, sent to show humans a better way to live.

Jesus is also the guardian of this new kingdom. It is a kingdom of great wealth, although not necessarily monetary wealth. It is a kingdom of great power, but not necessarily political or military power. It is a kingdom with one key resource, but there is more than enough of it for everyone. Paul calls this resource the good news.

The good news is that followers of Jesus are no longer subjects of the old law. Jesus fulfilled the law. People have been set free from the law. We are now free to love all people unconditionally and show kindness to them as Jesus has shown it to us. Jesus is the guardian of that truth similar to T'Challa being the guardian of the vibranium of Wakanda.

You

You have been entrusted with the good news. The reason Jesus is not here on earth is because he has entrusted the good news to his followers. They can hide it and try to preserve and protect it or they can share it. Paul says that he has been entrusted with the good news and in verse fourteen, he tells his readers that they also have been entrusted with the good news. God trusts you to let people know that they have been set free from the law. There is no religious class or caste entrusted with this message. There is no religious professional, like a priest or a prophet, entrusted with this message. God, through Jesus has given it to you.

It is difficult to share this good news when we are not sure it is good at all. Too often we feel trapped by the idea of the Law, trapped by the idea that we have to placate God's anger, or trapped by the fear that we are offensive to God. Feeling trapped is not good news. Being afraid is not good news. Understanding the freedom that comes with the good news is where we must begin.

What powers do you have to be an ambassador of good news to the people you know? First, you have superhuman endurance and stamina. Paul writes about his suffering, but within his suffering he continues to share the good news. The good news is why he is in prison. He told people they didn't have to follow the law anymore, that they didn't need a priest to slaughter animals on their behalf to appease God, and that they didn't have to be circumcised. Instead, he says they are free to show kindness to everyone, even their enemies. They can love people unconditionally, whether they are Jewish or not. Paul says he is suffering because of these ideas, but he has superhuman stamina and endurance. You have it too.

At times when life seems difficult, remember that God has given you the power to endure the suffering as long as the suffering is brought on because of the good news. When people are calling you names or belittling you because you are telling them about the good news and they do not understand it, know that you can withstand it.

You are a messenger of the good news. Your job is not to change people's lives or even to convince them of the good news. Your job is to share the good news with them. They can make their own decisions about it. You do not bear any of the responsibility for what people do with the message, but you do have a responsibility to share the message. If you are not using your powers to share this message of love, kindness, and freedom with people then you are hiding your vast wealth and resources from a world that desperately needs what you have.

Paul goes on to write that his readers have the power of the Holy Spirit in them to share the good news. Do not get too worried about what that means. You have the spirit of God in you. You have the image of God imprinted on you. Because of the power of God in you, the image of God in you, you can share this good news with people freely. You can demonstrate God's love and kindness to them.

You are an heir to the kingdom of God. You will inherit eternal life because Jesus created eternal life. In 1 Corinthians 13, Paul writes that things are difficult to understand now, but when we enter God's kingdom, we will know as we are fully known (13:12). Until then, he writes, three things remain, faith, hope, and love. The greatest of these is love (v13). Faith to believe that this life of love is worthwhile. Hope that God's kingdom will be even more spectacular than you imagine. And an ability to love people. This is greater than any mineral or resource in the world. You are an heir to that kingdom.

With that promise for eternal life comes a responsibility to represent that kingdom everywhere you go. You are an ambassador of love and kindness. Every step you take, every store you walk into, every day you are at work, every minute you spend with your family, you represent this kingdom. That puts some pressure on for sure.

You are an example of God's kindness to the rest of the world. More than that, you are a protector of God's kindness. So, you have to help people understand kindness and love. Remind other followers of Jesus to be kind, to speak kindly, and to love unconditionally. You now need to protect the image of God that is in you as well as the image of God that is in others. You do that by showing people kindness even if, or when, they are being unkind and unloving.

Finally, you are a protector of the good news. Do not let people tell you it is something other than it is. Do not let anyone try to convince you that you have to go back to following the Law or their laws or rules. It is your job to protect the good news. If you need to learn more about it, then learn more. If you need a mentor to show you how, then find one. In verse 14, Paul says to protect the good news that has been entrusted to you. The good news matters. It will make a difference in your life. It will change people. It can change the world! Be an exemplar of God's love and kindness.

About the Author

Darin Simms is the pastor at Union Grove BIC Church in Nappanee, Indiana with more than thirty years of ministry experience. He is married to Lori and together they have five children: Josiah, Bethany, Abigail, Hannah, and Noah and two grandchildren: Aubrey and Hailey. He has studied at Huntington University, Ashland Theological Seminary, Anabaptist Mennonite Biblical Seminary, and the University of Phoenix School for Advanced Studies.

He is an avid runner with numerous races under his belt including a Dopey Challenge, an Infinity Gauntlet Challenge, and a Coast to Coast Challenge from RunDisney. Running the Infinity Gauntlet Challenge with superheroes in Disneyland is still one of the highlights of his running experiences.

To contact Darin please find him online at:

www.darinsimms.com

www.facebook.com/darin.simms.7

www.pinterest.com/mrdarin

www.instagram.com/mrdarin1984

www.my.bible.com/users/mssimms